After You

Maryalicia Post

Illustrated by Ben Ecclestone

SOUVENIR PRESS

February

This is the last night I will watch you sleep
This is the last night
This is
Death closer than I
Drops of water more compassionate
Than kisses
I am your twin caught in the womb
You were called first
Helpless, you leave me
Through my final whisper
Your first silence
Only my heart beats
Heartless

March

Like a kite's tail whipped in the wind
One word snaps behind each thought:
Never
Cold morning alone in our bed
No memories coming
Let me in
Once you called me by my name in the
ordinary way
For the last time
When?
You were the benchmark for my distances
How will I find home
Again

April

First warm day since your going
Spring flowers mindlessly blossom
Such confusion
First rain since you left
You would have said 'the farmers need it'
Such silence
Outlived by daffodils, shoes, jobs begun
Mortality rules
Okay

May

Anxious for morning
I run towards it in the dark
And fall heavily
When dawn comes in its own time
I'll have bruises to show
For my haste

June

Sometimes now the fog lifts
And I see the shore
But my boat has no oars
And days are sails which fail to catch the
wind
I'll sleep
The tide must turn soon

July

Am I me or you? I can't remember
This food
Your favourite or mine?
Here's an equation;
When two become one
Take away one leaves zero

August

Six months now
Still yearning, still learning
Still running, still falling
Still here
Each night inventing the courage
To cross the dark doorsill
Into sleep

September

How portable grief is
I carry mine like a music box
And play
Its thin sharp melody
In all the silent places
Of the day

October

You belong to the sea now
Ashes dissolved
Like salt in the water
But when I search for you
It's the sky my eyes implore
To give you back

November

Since my heart became an orphan
Kindly people
Offer it shelter
They move chairs closer
At the table of their days
To make room for it
A grateful guest
It longs to feel better
If only for its host's sake

December

Walking from the shops
In windy dark
Frozen dinner bagged in plastic
Suddenly, for no reason,
Joy stirs in its sleep
I sense
Brightness
Like the first bead of water
Swelling from a rusty tap

January

The snowdrops you planted
For me
Are blooming again in the garden

Typeset by FiSH Books, Enfield, Middx.

Printed by
Tien Wah Press, Singapore

Exodus

That Rock was Christ

ISBN No: 1-905975-08-2

Published by Biblical Frameworks

Reg. Office: St Paul's Church, Robert Adam Street, London W10 3HW

Cover design, typesetting and production management by Verité CM Ltd, Worthing, West Sussex UK +44 (0) 1903 241975

Illustrations by Richard Thomas

Printed in England

Biblical Frameworks is registered in England No: 5712581
Charity No: 1116805.

Exodus

Contents

The Law

1 Introductory thoughts from Paul Blackham

The longest chapter in the Bible is all about… the Bible! Psalm 119 is all about the wonder of the Word of God. Verse 103 shows us the heart of someone who really loved the Bible. He cries out to the LORD God:

Psalm 119:103 – "How sweet are your words to my taste, sweeter than honey to my mouth!"

Whether you are reading the Bible alone or in some kind of group with others, expect to be thrilled by the words of the Living God. This is not like reading any other book. When we read and study the Bible the ultimate Author can be present with you, showing you His words and applying them to you.

Thousands of small groups are starting up all over the world – but what is it that is going to sustain them? It has to be the Bible.

So often, people don't quite know what to do with these small groups. Meeting together, sharing testimonies and experiences or sharing the odd verse is ultimately too sparse a diet to sustain people's spiritual needs in the long run, and really help them to grow.

What is needed is confidence in the Bible, and the ability to go to a book of the Bible rather than just an isolated verse. Each book of the Bible was written with a purpose, and it is only as we digest it as a book that we understand the real message, purpose, direction, storyline and characters.

It's a lot easier than people often think. You might think, "Oh, I can't manage a whole book of the Bible", but what we're trying to do in Book by Book is to break it down and show that it's straightforward.

The Bible was written not for specialists, not for academics – it was written for the regular believers down the ages.

The world is in desperate need for answers. How can the world live at peace? How can we live together with justice and truth and compassion? There are so many religions and so much division and bloodshed: what is the real and living way that takes us to the Living God who can give us all a new beginning?

The Bible is the answer from the Living God to all our questions.

Our desire is that many Christians would experience the joy and confidence in the Scriptures that is found throughout Psalm 119 – "How sweet are your words to my taste, sweeter than honey to my mouth!"

2 All about Book by Book

A. WHAT IS BOOK BY BOOK?

Book by Book is a Bible Study resource with accompanying DVD. It has been designed principally for use in small groups, but can also be used for study or larger group situations.

B. THE STRUCTURE OF BOOK BY BOOK

The Study Guide

The study guide provides the following features for each section of study:

- A Key Truth to focus on the most important truth in that section of the Bible Book.
- A Mind-Map diagram giving an overview of the study.
- An explanation of the Bible text, divided under suitable headings.
- A Bible Study, with detailed questions, designed to lead the individual or group deeper into the text.
- Further Questions, to stimulate deeper thought and discussion.
- A week of suggested daily Bible readings to fill out and explore the themes from the study.
- A Bible Study answers section at the back of the study guide, for extra help if need be.

The DVD

Key features provided on each DVD are as follows:

- There is a 15 minute discussion on the DVD linked to each section of the Study Guide Bible passage
- The on-screen host is Richard Bewes, with co-host Paul Blackham. A specially invited guest joins them in the Bible discussions.

C. SOME TIPS ON HOW TO USE BOOK BY BOOK

The beauty of Book by Book is that it offers not only great Biblical depth, but also flexibility of approach to study. Whether you are preparing to lead a small groups or to study alone you will find many options open to you.

And it doesn't matter if you are a new Christian or more experienced at leading Bible studies, Book by Book can be adapted to your situation. You don't need to be a specially trained leader.

Group study: preparing

- Select your study (preferably in the order of the book!)
- Watch the DVD programmes
- Read the commentary
- Use the suggested Bible questions...
- ...or formulate your own questions (the mind maps and key truths are a great guide for question structure)

Group study: suggested session structure

We recommend you set aside about an hour for each study

- 5 minutes – read the relevant section of the Bible
- 15 minutes – Watch the DVD programme
- 30 minutes – work through the Bible study questions (either your own or the ones in the guide), allowing time for discussion
- 10 minutes – If the study got the group thinking about wider issues of life today, Then consider the Further Questions to stimulate a broader discussion
- Taking it further – Suggest that group members look at some of the Daily Readings to follow up on the theme of the study

Given the volume of material you may even choose to take two weeks per study – using the DVD to generate discussion for one week and the Bible Study questions for the next.

Individual study

There is no set way to conduct study – here are some ideas:

- Select your study (preferably in the order of the book!)

- Read the Bible passage and related commentary.

- Try looking at the Mind-Map diagrams and seeing how the book has a structure.

- Take a look at the Key Truths and decide if they are the same conclusions you had reached when you read the book.

- Perhaps focus on the week of daily Bible reading to help you to explore the rest of the Bible's teaching on the themes of each section of study.

- Work through the Bible Questions. Don't worry if you get stuck, there is an 'answers' section at the back of the guide!

I will make you like God

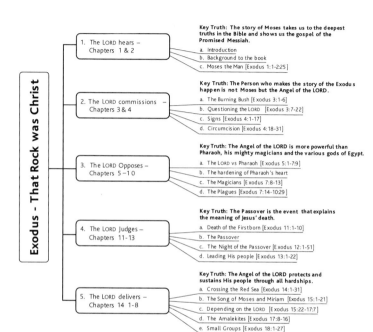

Exodus – That Rock was Christ

1. The LORD hears – Chapters 1 & 2

Key Truth: The story of Moses takes us to the deepest truths in the Bible and shows us the gospel of the Promised Messiah.

a. Introduction
b. Background to the book
c. Moses the Man [Exodus 1:1-2:25]

2. The LORD commissions – Chapters 3 & 4

Key Truth: The Person who makes the story of the Exodus happen is not Moses but the Angel of the LORD.

a. The Burning Bush [Exodus 3:1-6]
b. Questioning the LORD [Exodus 3:7-22]
c. Signs [Exodus 4:1-17]
d. Circumcision [Exodus 4:18-31]

3. The LORD Opposes – Chapters 5 – 10

Key Truth: The Angel of the LORD is more powerful than Pharaoh, his mighty magicians and the various gods of Egypt.

a. The LORD vs Pharaoh [Exodus 5:1-7:9]
b. The hardening of Pharaoh's heart
c. The Magicians [Exodus 7:8-13]
d. The Plagues [Exodus 7:14-10:29]

4. The LORD Judges – Chapters 11-13

Key Truth: The Passover is the event that explains the meaning of Jesus' death.

a. Death of the Firstborn [Exodus 11:1-10]
b. The Passover
c. The Night of the Passover [Exodus 12:1-51]
d. Leading His people [Exodus 13:1-22]

5. The LORD delivers – Chapters 14 1-8

Key Truth: The Angel of the LORD protects and sustains His people through all hardships.

a. Crossing the Red Sea [Exodus 14:1-31]
b. The Song of Moses and Miriam [Exodus 15:1-21]
c. Depending on the LORD [Exodus 15:22-17:7]
d. The Amalekites [Exodus 17:8-16]
e. Small Groups [Exodus 18:1-27]

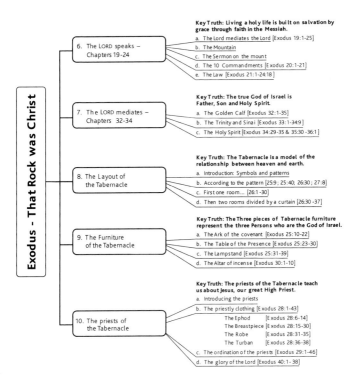

Exodus – That Rock was Christ

6. The LORD speaks – Chapters 19-24

Key Truth: Living a holy life is built on salvation by grace through faith in the Messiah.

a. The Lord mediates the Lord [Exodus 19:1-25]
b. The Mountain
c. The Sermon on the mount
d. The 10 Commandments [Exodus 20:1-21]
e. The Law [Exodus 21:1-24:18]

7. The LORD mediates – Chapters 32-34

Key Truth: The true God of Israel is Father, Son and Holy Spirit.

a. The Golden Calf [Exodus 32:1-35]
b. The Trinity and Sinai [Exodus 33:1-34:9]
c. The Holy Spirit [Exodus 34:29-35 & 35:30 -36:1]

8. The Layout of the Tabernacle

Key Truth: The Tabernacle is a model of the relationship between heaven and earth.

a. Introduction: Symbols and patterns
b. According to the pattern [25:9 ; 25:40; 26:30 ; 27:8]
c. First one room... [26:1 -30]
d. Then two rooms divided by a curtain [26:30 -37]

9. The Furniture of the Tabernacle

Key Truth: The Three pieces of Tabernacle furniture represent the three Persons who are the God of Israel.

a. The Ark of the covenant [Exodus 25:10-22]
b. The Table of the Presence [Exodus 25:23-30]
c. The Lampstand [Exodus 25:31-39]
d. The Altar of incense [Exodus 30:1-10]

10. The priests of the Tabernacle

Key Truth: The priests of the Tabernacle teach us about Jesus, our great High Priest.

a. Introducing the priests
b. The priestly clothing [Exodus 28:1-43]
   The Ephod   [Exodus 28:6-14]
   The Breastpiece [Exodus 28:15-30]
   The Robe   [Exodus 28:31-35]
   The Turban   [Exodus 28:36-38]
c. The ordination of the priests [Exodus 29:1-46]
d. The glory of the Lord [Exodus 40:1- 38]

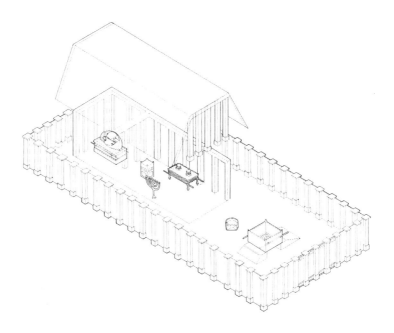

The Tabernacle

Study 1 The LORD hears

EXODUS CHAPTERS 1 & 2

Key Truth: The story of Moses takes us to the deepest truths in
the Bible and shows us the Gospel of the Promised Messiah.

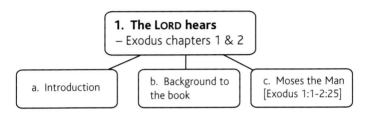

1. The LORD hears
— Exodus chapters 1 & 2

a. Introduction

b. Background to
the book

c. Moses the Man
[Exodus 1:1-2:25]

a. Introduction

Why study the book of Exodus when we have the New Testament?

Exodus could be called the *theological* book of the Bible.

The book of Exodus provides the theological framework for the rest of
the Bible.

Genesis set the scene for the whole Bible — but Exodus maps out the
theological logic, the doctrinal details of the Bible.

The story of the people of God being rescued from Egypt through the
judgement of God is a foundation pattern for the way in which they
looked forward to the Messiah delivering them from the power of sin and
the devil. As they saw how He redeemed them from Egypt, so they were
strengthened in their faith in Him to redeem them from sin, death and
the devil.

Jesus died at the Feast of Passover. This is a very significant part of the
death of Jesus and its meaning is established by the events of the book

of Exodus. The death of Jesus rests upon the book of Exodus for its theological explanation.

The entire creation, in both its aspects – heaven and earth – is explained by the framework given in the book of Exodus. We understand how the heavens and the earth relate, how sin has affected this relationship and how they will be redeemed, as we study the Tabernacle later on in Exodus.

The Tabernacle is the single most important building that the world has ever known, because it is the building that maps out the whole of reality to us. We understand the universe because of it.

Exodus gives us a wonderful presentation of the doctrine of the Trinity. As we see the Angel of God redeeming His people we are given a clear picture of the roles of the Father, Son and Holy Spirit.

When we look back at how the Christians of earlier generations understood the book of Exodus, we are shown the great depths of this majestic book of Moses. Matthew Henry tells us that it shows us the forming of the children of Israel into a church, and "shadows forth the state of the church, in the wilderness of this world, until her arrival at the heavenly Canaan".

While we are thinking of those older Christian books, you will find the Old Testament people of God referred to as 'the Church'. Some people find this strange because they are used to thinking of 'church' as a New Testament word only. However, speaking of the Church in the Old Testament is true to Scripture because several times in Exodus in the ancient Greek translation of the Old Testament, called the Septuagint, the Israelite community is called '*ekklesia*' (the Greek word for 'church').

The events of this book and the fulfilment of the many prophecies made to Abraham which we will see unfold here did not happen in a secret place. They occupied centre-stage in world history. We are reminded that these events were the topic of discussion in all the surrounding nations of the world (Exodus 32:12,25). The events of Exodus often made the news headlines every day.

This is a book that demands our attention. If we can grasp something of the "Exodus treasure chest" we will find our understanding of the world, the Bible and life is taken to a new level.

b. Background to the book

'Exodus' is simply the Latin form of Greek 'ex hodos' meaning 'exit' or 'going out'.

It is clear that Exodus immediately follows on from Genesis. The Hebrew title for 'Exodus' (*we'elleh shemoth*, Lit., 'And these are the names of') is the same phrase that appears in Genesis 46:8.

The book begins by summarizing what has happened since the end of Genesis. From being the most popular people in Egypt, creators of the state of Egypt and the power of the Pharaoh through Joseph, the Church had become despised and persecuted, subject to harsh working conditions. Later on, during their wanderings in the wilderness, they longed to return to Egypt (Num 11:5 for example), but the Bible makes it clear that slavery, whether in Egypt or in sin, is terrible.

The new king was an ignorant, arrogant fool, v 8-9. We are not even told his name, even though we are told the names of two midwives. Although the Israelites had only done Egypt good, and benefited the nation, (see Genesis 47:20-27), he was suspicious of them in an entirely racist way. 'Pithom', where they lived, v 11, means "the fortress of foreigners".

However, verse 12, the more the Church was persecuted, the more it expanded. This expansion may not only have been through birth. There were also Egyptians who lived among the Israelites and we see marriages between Egyptians and Israelites (Leviticus 24:10).

The Church was definitely bringing foreigners in, and we will see that it was a racially international group that set out as the 'church in the wilderness'.

However, it is expansion due to procreation that Pharaoh decides to tackle first. He calls in the Hebrew midwives, whose names were Shiphrah (Beautiful) and Puah (Splendid). Pharaoh wanted them to murder all the baby boys. These two midwives must have been very busy servicing a population of some 2-3 million – the Israelites had grown in number from around 70 to 2-3 million, in 10 generations! This is perhaps why they were able to say what they did in verse 19. They must have been racing around from one home to another and we can see why they might be late arriving at the births given the pressure they must have been under! God approved of the midwives 'going slow' in civil disobedience and gave them plenty of babies of their own.

c. Moses the Man (Exodus 1:1-2:25)

Moses is the most humble man who has ever lived apart from Jesus, Numbers 12:3.

Why? Well, we need to appreciate how 'full of himself' he might have been. He had been in the family of Pharaoh, the ruler of the world's great superpower. It is possible that Moses could have become Pharaoh if he had that ambition. He received the best education that the world had to offer. Power, money, influence and prestige all belonged to him. In turning from that world, he became a prince in spiritual things. Moses had became a close friend of the Second Person of the Trinity, God the Son, Exodus 33:11, and was personally buried by Him, Deuteronomy 34:6. The Law, that provided the theological context for the next 1500 years of the Church, was given through him. Many people with less than 1% of Moses' experiences make careers out of telling their stories. However, Moses was amazingly humble and self-sacrificial.

The book of Exodus takes us through the first 80 years of this extraordinary man. We see him commissioned as an apostle of the Angel of the Lord and we see how he matures into the passionate administrator of the Law and the Tabernacle that he is in the book of Leviticus.

Amram, a member of the tribe of Levi, and descendant of Kohath, Exodus 6:20, had married Jochebed, who belonged to the same tribe. They had already had two children, Miriam and Aaron. The birth of their next child not only won their hearts, but seemed to point him out as destined of God for some special purpose – "He was no ordinary child", Acts 7:20.

Moses' mother saved him by casting him into the Nile (as ordered!), but placed him in an 'ark'. This is the same word in the Hebrew as the ark built by Noah. Just as Noah was delivered from the killing water by an ark, so is Moses. He is given his name which means 'Saved', because he had been 'saved' from the Nile. Where many boys were being thrown into the river to be killed, here is one drawn out to have life. There is so much similarity between the births of Moses and Jesus, particularly the massacre of the baby boys. However, to make the difference clear, he is not called Jesus (Saviour) but Moses (Saved).

As we noted, Moses was in the family of the leader of the world's super power. All the treasures of the world awaited him. All his worldly desires could be satisfied but he turned them all down for Christ (Hebrews 11:26).

Moses is often given a very bad press as being a murderer. Yet, this is not the way that the Bible presents him. We tend to see him as merely sinful when we read Exodus 2, yet in Acts 7:23-28 Stephen reminds us of the proper perspective to have as we read Exodus. Stephen shows us that Moses knew that he was the one sent to deliver the Church from the captivity of Egypt – even before the burning bush encounter where the Angel of the Lord tells him this. Perhaps Moses was assuming the Israelites would rise up and leave Egypt once he had begun the revolution! The fact that they didn't trust in what the Lord was doing through Moses meant that a whole generation of Israelites (40 years) had to remain in captivity to endure worse persecution. That pattern of '40 years punishment for sin' is played out in the Pentateuch, the first 5 books of the Bible. Nevertheless, Moses just can't help being a rescuer and a pastor, Exodus 2:19.

In 2:15, Moses runs away to the land of the Midianites – the very people who had taken Joseph down to Egypt in the first place. He meets Jethro, who is the priest of Midian. We are not told *how* Jethro is a priest when the Aaronic and Levitical priesthood had not yet been established, but we do know he is a man of great theological depth and wisdom.

The father-in-law of Moses worshipped the God of Abraham, as his name states: *Reuel*, the 'friend of El'. He became Moses' spiritual teacher through these 40 years. However, they seem to have been long years of depression for Moses. Although Zipporah bore a son, Moses betrayed his loneliness by naming his son Gershom, "I have become an alien in a foreign land", v 22 (Gershom means 'alien') .

From being at the top of the world to spending 40 years in the desert, leading sheep around, were there many times that he simply assumed that his life had been wasted, that the Lord had nothing for him to do?

Everything seems to be hopeless here for God's people. But, there is always hope with the God of Resurrection from the dead. Exodus 2:23-25.

Study 1	Bible Study Questions

Exodus chapter 1

1. Verses 1-7: The Israelites were living in Egypt and growing as a people there. How did they come to be there in the first place? (Genesis 47:11-12)

2. Verses 8-14: Joseph was the second most powerful and influential man in Egypt whilst he was alive, yet the new Pharaoh knew nothing of him. What does that tell us about fame and importance? What should we be aiming for in our lives?

3. Joseph is quickly forgotten in Egypt, however, he is remembered throughout the rest of the Bible and he is held as an example to Christians all over the world today. How can this be an encouragement as we live Christian lives in the world? What is the audience that we should really be concerned about.

4. Verses 15-21: What kind of danger do you think they were putting themselves into by disobeying Pharaoh? What does this tell us about the relationship the midwives had with the Lord?

5. As Christians, we will doubtless face many situations where our faith conflicts with what the world expects or demands from us. What can we learn about those kind of situations from the story of the midwives? How does the Lord look on such faith?

6. Verse 22: Can you see some similarities between the birth of Moses and the birth of Jesus in Matthew 2? In what ways would both Moses and Jesus lead their people out of slavery?

Study 1   Further Questions

1. How is it that God blessed the two Hebrew midwives when they lied to Pharaoh? Does this mean it is okay to lie so long as we have good intentions?

2. How could Jethro have been a priest? Is there any significance in the fact that he was a shepherd and a priest?

3. Why is it *ironic* that Moses calls his son 'Gershom' (alien)? What situation has he fled from?

Study 1   Daily Readings

Day 1	Genesis 47:11-31
Day 2	Exodus 1
Day 3	Exodus 2
Day 4	Matthew 2
Day 5	Acts 7:17-29
Day 6	Psalm 90 (a psalm of Moses)
Day 7	Hebrews 11

The daily Bible readings are an opportunity not only to read through all of the material in the book under study, but also to read parts of the Bible that relate to the themes and issues that we have been considering. We try to make sure that we receive light from the whole Bible as we think through the key issues each week.

The Bull Sacrifice

Study 2   The LORD commissions

Chapters 3-4

> **Key Truth:** The Person who makes the story of the Exodus happen is not Moses but the Angel of the LORD.

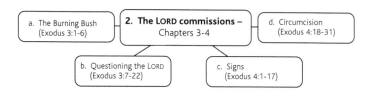

a. The Burning Bush
(Exodus 3:1-6)

2. The LORD commissions –
Chapters 3-4

d. Circumcision
(Exodus 4:18-31)

b. Questioning the LORD
(Exodus 3:7-22)

c. Signs
(Exodus 4:1-17)

a.   The Burning Bush (Exodus 3:1-6)

At 80 years of age after a 40-year long career as a shepherd, Moses probably would have been thinking of a retirement flat on the Mediterranean coast. However, the Angel of the Lord had more for him to do. He was not called 'Saved' for nothing.

Moses had done his shepherding at the mountain of God, Horeb, Exodus 3:1. On this mountain the Angel of the LORD appeared standing in flames of fire within a bush, a bush that was not consumed by this fire. The flames of fire indicate the barrier between heaven and earth, the barrier established in Genesis 3:23 when Adam and Eve were cast out of Eden. We will see this fiery boundary between heaven and earth many times in the book of Exodus... and in the rest of the Bible.

On the basis of Acts 7:30 it seems that at first Moses thought that this was simply *an* angel... perhaps this is why he did not remove his sandals as he approached: he was not yet fully aware of who he was meeting. Moses simply wanted to see why this angelic/spiritual fire did not burn up the bush; a fire that fuels itself!

The first thing the Angel of the LORD needed to do was make Moses aware of who he was speaking to. The Angel of the LORD reveals His identity to Moses – "I am the God of your father, the God of Abraham, the God of Isaac and the God of Jacob."

The Bible tells us Moses was afraid to *look at God*. This is a face-to-face encounter with Christ, the second Person of the Trinity.

> Not a created angel certainly; for he is called Jehovah, Exodus 3:4, expressive attributes of the Godhead applied to him, Exodus 3:14, Yet he is an angel, malach, a messenger, in whom was the name of God, Exodus 23:21; and in whom dwelt all the fulness of the Godhead bodily, Colossians 2:9; and who, in all these primitive times, was the Messenger of the covenant, Malachi 3:1. And who was this but JESUS, the Leader, Redeemer, and Saviour of mankind?[1]

Is it right to use the word 'Christ' in our study of the book of Exodus to identify the Promised One, the second Person of the Trinity? Some may feel that 'Christ' is a New Testament word which shouldn't be used in the Old Testament. This is quite mistaken. It is the Greek translation of the Hebrew word 'Messiah'. It is therefore an Old Testament term which is used in the New Testament. The New Testament is happy to use the word 'Christ' in its own studies of the Old Testament. See for example, 1 Corinthians 10:4, when the apostle Paul identifies the One who redeemed the ancient Israelites as Christ. We should always follow the examples of Bible study set out for us in the Bible! So in Hebrews 11:26, the author uses the word 'Christ' to name the One who was the object of Moses' faith and hope. Therefore, it seems right when we are studying the writings of Moses to follow the example of Hebrews 11 and identify the promised Mediator with one of His most common titles. The Jews for Jesus website is a treasure trove of Biblical studies on these issues[2].

---

[1] Adam Clarke's commentary on Exodus 3. See also Clarke on Genesis 16:7

[2] www.jewsforjesus.org There are lots of online papers and Bible studies at this site, particularly in the 'Believers' section. Some have said that we should not speak about Christ in the Old Testament because He is the mystery "which was not made known to men in other generations as it has now been revealed" (Ephesians 3:5). However, the very next verse of Ephesians 3 explains that the mystery is not Christ, but the way in which Israel was extended out to include Gentiles all over the world – "this mystery is that through the Gospel the Gentiles are heirs together with Israel, members together of one body, and sharers together in the promise in" Jesus the Messiah. We see the same explanation of this 'mystery' in Romans 16:26 – the truth about the Messiah in the prophetic writings is now being revealed to the whole world.

This is the first of many such encounters with this divine Mediator for Moses, but we should never forget how utterly stunning such an encounter was. Just because the Angel of the LORD can be seen, doesn't mean we should forget how overwhelming and even fatal it can be to see Him in His great glory. When the apostle John, who had seen Jesus first hand for three years, saw the glorious risen and ascended Christ in Revelation 1, he was very afraid.

b. Questioning the LORD (Exodus 3:7-22)

The first question in Moses mind must have been why the Angel of the LORD, the God of Abraham, Isaac and Jacob was there and what He had come to do. The answer is given in verses 7-10. In verse 8, the LORD says 'I have come down to rescue them..'. However, it is verse 10 that causes more worries. He is being commissioned as the one who will act as the ambassador of the Angel of the LORD to Pharaoh. Moses is to be the preacher of the Word to Pharaoh.

Moses isn't happy about this. In fact, we will see Moses still grumbling about this for the next three chapters. But isn't his reply strange? Moses answers back to God! How strange this must seem to the Angel of the LORD who is used to the angels carrying out His commands with awe, reverence and unquestioning obedience!

But the Angel of the LORD is patient with Moses and explains that he need have no fear because He would be with him. The Angel of the Lord was personally guaranteeing that all the people of Israel would be delivered out of Egypt to that very mountain.

Moses is still full of questions. Moses wants to know the Name and the identity of the Angel of the LORD.

The Lord's Name is: I AM WHO I AM – God is self-defined. The only One who can determine what He does or who He is… is Himself. He defines Himself. I AM WHO I AM – through all the storms of life with its emptiness, YHWH is the One whose existence is eternal, solid, always the same. He is our Rock who we can trust when we feel tossed about.

The great 18th century Bible scholar Matthew Henry explains this name of the LORD. If you can, take time to meditate on this part of Matthew Henry's commentary. There is real depth and treasure in these words:

A name that denotes *what he is in himself* (v. 14): *I am that I am.* This explains his name *Jehovah,* and signifies,

(1.) That he is self-existent; he has his being of himself, and has no dependence upon any other: the greatest and best man in the world must say, by the grace of God *I am what I am*; but God says absolutely – and it is more than any creature, man or angel, can say – I am that I am. Being self-existent, he cannot but be self-sufficient, and therefore all-sufficient, and the inexhaustible fountain of being and bliss.

(2.) That he is eternal and unchangeable, and always the same, yesterday, to-day, and for ever; he will be what he will be and what he is; see Rev. 1:8.

(3.) That we cannot by searching find him out… Do we ask what is God? Let it suffice us to know that he is what he is, what he ever was, and ever will be. *How little a portion is heard of him!* Job 26:14.

(4.) That he is faithful and true to all his promises, unchangeable in his word as well as in his nature, and not a man that he should lie. Let Israel know this, *I AM hath sent me unto you.*

2. A name that denotes *what he is to his people*. Lest that name *I AM* should amuse and puzzle them, he is further directed to make use of another name of God more familiar and intelligible: *The Lord God of your fathers hath sent me unto you* (v. 15): Thus God had made himself known to him (v. 6), and thus he must make him known to *them,*

(1.) That he might revive among them the religion of their fathers, which, it is to be feared, was much decayed and almost lost. This was necessary to prepare them for deliverance, Ps. 80:19.

(2.) That he might raise their expectations of the speedy performance of the promises made to their fathers. Abraham, Isaac, and Jacob, are particularly named, because with Abraham the covenant was first made, and with Isaac and Jacob often expressly renewed; and these three were distinguished from their brethren, and chosen to be the trustees of the covenant, when their brethren were rejected. God will have this to be his name for ever, and it has been, is, and will be, his name, by which his worshippers know him, and distinguish him from all false gods; see 1 Kings 18:36.

Note: God's covenant-relation to his people is what he will be ever mindful of, what he glories in, and what he will have us never forget, but give him the glory of.

Notice that the delegation of Moses and the elders are told to ask Pharaoh for a 'three-day journey' into the desert. This is not a request for just a week off work – three days to get there, one day to do the sacrificing and three days back! We will see the great significance a 'three day' experience has in the book of Exodus. A 'three day journey' seems to be a technical, theological term for a journey to personally meet with the LORD. They are certainly not implying that they will ever be coming back and Pharaoh clearly understands this. He tells them not to go far, 8:28.

c. Signs (Exodus 4:1-17)

Chapter 4 begins with Moses still unsure of his ground – how can he prove to the elders of Israel that he really has met the Angel of the LORD? Perhaps nobody had seen the Angel of the LORD for 400 years... why *now* and why to Moses?

Moses receives three signs to support his case:

- The staff which became a snake.
- The sign of the renewed flesh.
- The water into blood.

We will examine each of these in more detail in our Bible study, but we can simply note how important each of these symbols were. To have power over the serpent was so wonderful after the terrible events of Genesis chapter 3. To know that human corruption can be healed is such good news given the corruption of sin in our hearts and the curse of sin in our flesh. The water that was the power of Egypt in the Nile was also in the hands of the Living God.

From 4:10 Moses raises a whole new category of excuses, relating to his inability to speak eloquently – having spent 40 years as a shepherd, he may well have spent weeks without any human conversation. However, the Angel of the LORD had commissioned him. What more was there to say?

Surely Christ, the One through whom all things were created, knew all about Moses and what he could and couldn't do. He didn't want a man who would undermine the power of the Gospel with his own great eloquence or ability. He wanted a man who would trust in Him with absolute dependence and humility, v 12 "I will teach you". This is what salvation is all about.

At this stage in Moses' life he is not the man of great faith that he would later be. It is so encouraging to see that even at the age of 80, when patterns, habits and attitudes were so deeply ingrained, Moses can make such enormous strides in Christian discipleship.

However, here at Horeb Moses is not doing well. In verse 13 he directly calls the LORD's judgement into question – 'send someone else'. This angers the Angel of the LORD – but He doesn't reject Moses. He lets Aaron be an assistant to Moses to do the speaking that Moses seemed so fearful of doing.

d. Circumcision (Exodus 4:18-31)

In 4:24-26 we see how Moses is given a defining experience. The rest of his life would centre on the correct and careful performance of the signs and shadows of the Gospel that would be given at Sinai. He had to be a man who was passionately committed to 'sacramental order'. In other words, he had to care very deeply whether everything was being done exactly as the LORD had commanded.

The Angel of the LORD was angry with Moses, because he had failed to circumcise his son. This was very serious. The terms of this Gospel sign had been perfectly clear back in Genesis 17 – every male member of the household was to be circumcised on the 8th day.

Why had Moses failed to do this? Had he over-spiritualised the Gospel? Did Moses assume that such a messy sign didn't apply to his family? The LORD comes to kill him because of this. There is no pretence in this threat – such a disobedient view of Gospel signs really can provoke this kind of reaction. We know how the Corinthian church suffered fatalities over their own inadequate view of the Lord's Supper – 1 Cor. 11:29-32.

Zipporah, his Gentile wife, knew what to do. She performed an emergency circumcision and touched the LORD's feet with her son's [foreskin].

When this sign of blood is offered to the Angel of the LORD, He relents from His desire to kill Moses. Zipporah worships Him as her Bridegroom of Blood.[3]

Chapter 4 ends with such a contrast to Moses' insecurity and hesitation. Aaron hears all about what had happened and simply gathers the elders together. He speaks to them for Moses, the miraculous signs are duly performed and without any questions or doubts the people bow down and worship the Angel of the LORD.

---

[3] The NIV and many other translations give the impression that Zipporah touched Moses' feet with her son's [foreskin]. Why such an action would prevent the Angel of the LORD from killing Moses is not clear.

Study 2   Bible Study Questions

Exodus 4:1-17

There are deep truths in the 3 signs given to Moses by the Angel of the LORD. Each of them shows aspects of the grace and power of the Lord.

1. Verses 2-3: What could the snake represent in this first sign? Remember Genesis 3. Over what does this sign show the Lord has total power? What does this mean for the world and humanity?

2. Verse 4: How does the LORD's instruction to pick up the snake by its tail further demonstrate the power of the LORD? (see also Mark 16:15-18)

3. Verses 6-7: The NIV translates this as 'cloak', but it is literally 'heart' or 'chest'. Moses was to put his hand over his heart. With this in mind, what could the leprosy and its healing be a picture of? (Jeremiah 17:9 and Ezekiel 11:19-20)

4. Verse 9: The Nile would have been a great source of life to the Egyptians, but for those who disobey the LORD, it is turned into death/blood. How does this compare with what the LORD gives to those who love and obey Him? See Revelation 22:1-2 and John 4:10-14.

5. Verses 11-17: How are these verses both an encouragement and a warning in our Christian lives?

Study 2   Further Questions

1. In Exodus 3:12 the Angel of the Lord gives Moses a sign that the people will be brought back to that very mountain. Does this ever happen? If so, when?

2. Exodus 3:21-22 are important verses describing how the treasures of Egypt were plundered in the Exodus. What connection does this have with Psalm 68:18 which talks of the great triumph of the cross?

3. What is the meaning of circumcision? This might seem a strange practice to some or to others it has merely medical significance. However, what is the *Gospel truth* shown in this activity? See Deut 10:16 and Deut 30:6 for Moses' own explanation.

Study 2   Daily Readings

Day 1	Exodus 3
Day 2	Exodus 4
Day 3	Acts 7:30-53
Day 4	Hebrews 3
Day 5	Psalm 99
Day 6	Luke 5:12-16 & John 18:1-11
Day 7	Acts 28:1-10

The daily Bible readings are an opportunity not only to read through all of the material in the book under study, but also to read parts of the Bible that relate to the themes and issues that we have been considering. We try to make sure that we receive light from the whole Bible as we think through the key issues each week.

The Plagues

Study 3   The LORD opposes

Exodus chapters 5-10

> **Key Truth:** The Angel of the LORD is more powerful than Pharaoh, his mighty magicians and the various gods of Egypt.

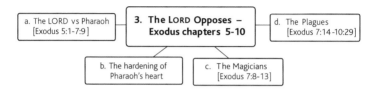

a.   The LORD vs Pharaoh (Exodus 5:1-7:9)

The bulk of chapter 5 is taken up with the working conditions of the Church under Pharaoh. It is a harsh regime. This Pharaoh seems to have lost his grip on reality. He is power mad. His reaction to the first confrontation with Moses and Aaron "Who is the Lord that I should obey Him?" is frighteningly arrogant. However, it is the purpose of the Exodus – that all the world, Israelite and non-Israelite, will know of the Lord's Name.

The Pharaoh of Exodus 4 has long forgotten his debt to the LORD and the Church (Genesis 47:20-27). He simply wants to get as much work as he possibly can from them. His demands are unreasonable and he constantly assumes that the Israelites are simply lazy. Perhaps he is jealous of their possession of the land of Goshen (Genesis 47:5-6). Thus, chapter 5 ends in a sorry state with the Israelites being forced to work harder than before. Moses seems to have made things even worse.

Is this experience allowed so that there can be no doubts that the Church *must* be redeemed from Egypt? They have no possible future in such a place.

After reassurance from the LORD, there comes a strange speech in 6:2-3. At first glance this looks as if the Name Yahweh was unknown to everybody before this point. This is definitely not the case as the Name

Yahweh is known by the very earliest humans – Genesis 4:1 & 26. Abraham, Isaac and Jacob all use the name 'Yahweh' (L<small>ORD</small>) in the book of Genesis. The simplest explanation seems to be the way the verse has been translated. In the NIV translation there is a footnote which acknowledges the alternative, and much more reasonable, translation: "by my Name the L<small>ORD</small> did I not make Myself known to them?"

The L<small>ORD</small> wants them to know that He is the same one who was known by Abraham, Isaac and Jacob, the One who cared for them and made Gospel promises to them.

We end chapter 6 having seen the care and patience that the Angel of the L<small>ORD</small> has invested into commissioning His apostle Moses. With great love and kindness He has addressed many of Moses' anxieties, and established the credibility of Moses in the hearts and minds of Israel. However, the preparation ends with Moses too insecure to go and address Pharaoh for himself, (6:29-7:9). Aaron would have to be the mouthpiece of Moses – at least to begin with.

b. The hardening of Pharaoh's heart

It is useful for us to take a moment to consider something that often troubles people as they study the book of Exodus – the way that the L<small>ORD</small> hardens Pharaoh's heart so that he does not respond to Moses.

The Lord does not take Pharaoh's *soft* heart and make it *hard*. Rather, Pharaoh hardens his own heart, and the Lord further hardens it as a punishment for this.

In Exodus 9:34, Pharaoh sins by hardening his heart and straight afterwards in 10:1, we are told for the first time (after 6 plagues!) that the Lord has hardened his heart.

In Romans 1:21-32, we are told that the Lord does this with *all* people who choose wickedness. No one stays the same after hearing the Gospel. Either you believe or you are hardened.

Each plague is an opportunity and exhortation to Pharaoh to repent. In 8:9, Pharaoh agrees to let the Israelites go. But the answer he gives is "tomorrow" which seems quite strange. Why not today? Scripture tells us that the Spirit constantly says "*Today* if you hear His voice do not harden your heart", Psalm 95:11

By the time we reach the 8th plague in chapter 10, all references to Pharaoh's hardening of heart is accredited to the LORD. This is a terrible thing. Pharaoh has had his chance and remained unwilling. Now the Lord uses him in *judgement* to serve His purpose of salvation for all nations by making His Name, Yahweh, great.

c. The Magicians (Exodus 7:8-13)

The first sign that the Lord gives to Pharaoh and his officials is in 7:8-13, where Aaron's staff becomes a snake. Although the magicians can replicate this sign, Aaron's staff swallows up theirs.

We need to see the spiritual significance of this. If the serpents perhaps symbolise spiritual and magical power, the magicians assumed that they were the masters of the occult world of the spirits and the gods. The devil granted them real power and they assumed it was the greatest power. However, the power of the Living God over the powers and principalities of this world is absolute. They are a footstool for His feet.

Moses demonstrated that the LORD God of Abraham, Isaac and Jacob is the Creator of the heavens and the earth… and the gods of Egypt are no gods at all.

It is interesting to note that the plagues which the magicians are able to replicate (water into blood and the frogs) are the very plagues make the land of Egypt stink. See 7:18 for blood, and 8:13-14 for the frogs, which die and stink in the land.

To copy these doesn't do any good at all! Why not *undo* them?

d. The Plagues (Exodus 7:14-10:29)

The plagues serve as an important demonstration of the great and terrible judgements the Lord must exercise in order to redeem us from slavery. We are told that the Lord is making His Name known to the Israelites (6:7), to Pharaoh (7:17), to all the earth (9:16), and to the Israelite descendants to come (10:2). This includes *us*.

So the Exodus and the judgements are in fact a sign to everybody at every time that Yahweh is the Lord and that all who reject Him will suffer terrible judgement.

Let us take a brief look at each plague and take note of what each one teaches us.

Water into Blood, 7:14-25 – This plague comes about by the staff striking the Nile – the very place where the slaughtering of the Hebrew babies took place. Indeed, Moses himself should have been dead in that very river.

Frogs, 8:1-15 – Aaron stretches his staff over the waters of Egypt to produce frogs. This is the plague from the water. In Revelation 16:13-14 we are shown the symbolic connection between demons and frogs, so this plague perhaps is a statement of Egypt being over-run with demons.

Gnats/Lice, 8:16-19 – When the Lord creates gnats/lice in 8:16-17 from the dust of the ground, the magicians cannot replicate this and acknowledge that it was the finger of God, v19. The last time we heard of something living being created from the dust was in Genesis 2:7 when the Lord created man. It is only He who can make dust become a living thing.

Flies, 8:20-32 – Here a distinction is made between what happens to Egypt and what happens to Israel, see 8:23. It is therefore an opportunity for everyone to repent and join Israel for safety from judgement.

Death of livestock, 9:1-7 – The Lord increases the severity and impact of the plagues to the taking of animal life. Pharaoh sends men to investigate the Israelite animals to see if they have died, v7. He has understood what is going on, but still refuses to let them go.

Boils, 9:8-12 – Now humans begin to suffer from the plagues. The soot which Moses throws from a furnace into the air which becomes fine dust all over the land is a symbol of great judgement. The Hebrew word for 'furnace' is used again only twice in the Bible, also in situations of judgement, Genesis 19:28 and Exodus 19:18.

Hail, 9:13-35 – This time it is Moses not Aaron who stretches out the staff to bring down the hail. It seems as if he is getting more confident and now seems to be willing to act as the Lord initially wanted him to. As we go on with Moses, we see that he does become excellent at speaking to the people and does not continue to use Aaron. See Deuteronomy 32 for Moses' glorious finale.

Locusts, 10:1-20 – The Spirit brings the locusts (the Hebrew word *Ruah* can be translated Spirit). This time, Pharaoh agrees that the male Israelites can go. However, this is totally unacceptable to the Lord because He redeems everyone, not just the men.

Darkness, 10:21-29 – It seems like a very unusual kind of darkness – one which could be felt. No one was able to see anyone else or leave his house. Egypt has become a fruitless, dark, barren, ruined place before the Lord. This is the result of rejecting Him. As we approach the death of the firstborn in Egypt, this darkness covers the land for 3 days. When the firstborn of God the Father was killed, darkness then covered the land for 3 hours, Matthew 27:45. Thus, darkness is the ultimate sign of God's judgement.

Study 3   Bible Study Questions

Exodus 5:1-6:1

Moses and Aaron, two men 80 and 83 years of age, are sent to face the great king of Egypt with nothing but a stick in their hands. This truly is a time of faith and not works.

1. Verse 1: Here Moses and Aaron meet Pharaoh to challenge him to obey the LORD. Remember why Pharaoh is such a powerful leader in the world (Genesis 47:20-27). Why does this make his opposition to the LORD so wicked?

2. Verses 2-3: How is this confrontation with Pharaoh an evangelistic encounter? How do Moses and Aaron present the LORD to him?

3. Verse 10: Compare the announcement of Pharaoh's message in verse 10 with the announcement of the LORD's message in verse 1. Notice the word 'Go'. What are the differences between the messages themselves and what does this tell us about Pharaoh and the LORD?

4. Verses 15-20: Are the Israelites more concerned with the LORD's priorities or with Pharaoh's? Whose people do they see themselves as? (look at v16)

5. How can the bad example of the Israelites' lack of faith in the Angel of the LORD challenge us to act positively through difficult times?

6. Verse 21: The Israelites are being harshly treated by the world. Compare 5:21 with what Paul says in 2 Corinthians 2:14-16. How can these verses help us understand the reasons why the world treats us badly?

Study 3   Further Questions

1. According to Romans 9:17-18, why did the LORD harden Pharaoh's heart? Did it work? Do we find evidence that the other nations heard about what happened in the Exodus? Keep an eye out for such references as you read through the books of Moses.

2. How could Moses simply walk out of the city during the worst hailstorm Egypt had ever seen and not be harmed? (9:33) Why?

3. Are there any similarities between the plagues of Egypt and the plagues in Revelation chapter 16?

Study 3   Daily Readings

Day 1	Exodus 5
Day 2	Exodus 6
Day 3	Exodus 7
Day 4	Exodus 8
Day 5	Exodus 9
Day 6	Exodus 10
Day 7	Psalm 105

The daily Bible readings are an opportunity not only to read through all of the material in the book under study, but also to read parts of the Bible that relate to the themes and issues that we have been considering. We try to make sure that we receive light from the whole Bible as we think through the key issues each week.

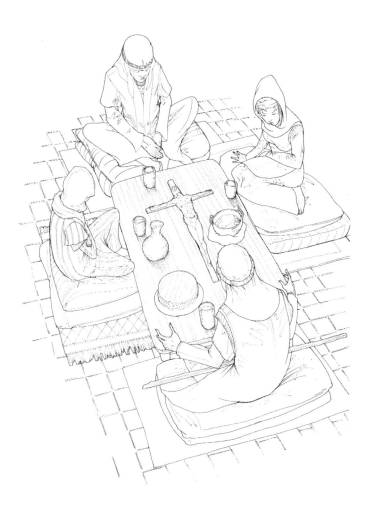

Passover

Study 4   The LORD judges

Exodus 11-13

> **Key Truth:** The Passover is the event that explains the meaning of Jesus' death.

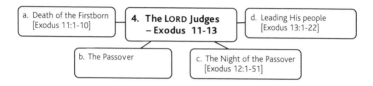

a. Death of the Firstborn [Exodus 11:1-10]

4. The LORD Judges – Exodus 11-13

d. Leading His people [Exodus 13:1-22]

b. The Passover

c. The Night of the Passover [Exodus 12:1-51]

a.   Death of the Firstborn (Exodus 11:1-10)

Each of Pharaoh's refusals had brought a terrible plague on Egypt and now the road to judgement had reached its destination. There was no more time, no more patience for Pharaoh. The Living LORD is slow to anger, but not infinitely so.

Pharaoh's utter contempt for the Word of the LORD and his refusal to see Moses ever again, brings everything to its conclusion. Judgement day arrives as the LORD pronounces this final plague upon Egypt.

Moses was hot with anger as he announced this plague and turned away from Pharaoh, 11:8. Moses was in full harmony with the LORD, who could no longer endure Pharaoh's unbelief. There would be no more warnings – now Christ Himself, the Avenging LORD, comes to Egypt to mete out judgement.

This time it was to be more personal and more terrible than anything before – verse 4. Egypt had been a nation divided between the rulers and the ruled, the slave and the free, but on the day of judgement everybody was the same. All fell under the judgement of God, whether royal or beggar.

Just as in Revelation 6:16 the world must face the wrath of Christ the Lamb on Judgement Day itself, so on this prophetic judgement day in Exodus, it is Christ the LORD Himself who comes to deliver judgement.

Moses is not told to stretch out his hand to bring a plague. Instead, he must run for cover, just as all those who feared the Word of the LORD had to do – run for cover, as the Angel of the LORD passed through Egypt in terrible judgement.

Yet, even this final plague does not bring *total* destruction. Those firstborn would have to bear the judgement of God alone on behalf of the whole nation. The firstborn were substitutes for the whole nation.

Way back in Exodus chapter 4 the Angel of the LORD had known it would end in this way – 4:21-23. The Angel of the LORD describes Israel as His own firstborn son... but it is He Himself who is *THE* Firstborn Son of the Father. Israel, the Church, is God's firstborn by adoption, but the Angel of the LORD, God the Son, the Eternal Christ, is God's Firstborn Son eternally and by nature.

When the Angel of the LORD said that it was the *firstborn* who must bear the anger of God's judgement, He was not speaking dispassionately, at a distance. In saying this, He prophesies His own death sentence.

Psalm 89 is an amazing Messianic psalm and in verse 27 we see that the Messiah is the firstborn.

In Genesis 3:15 it had been clear that Christ must suffer to redeem the world. In Genesis 22, Abraham had prophesied that the Messiah, the Lamb of God, would die as an atoning sacrifice on Mount Moriah.[4] Here in Exodus Christ's identity as the firstborn of the Father, the firstborn over all creation, is brought to the fore. It is the Firstborn who alone can stand in the place of judgement for others. As *the* Firstborn He would bear the sins of the whole world as the Divine substitute on the Cross.

b. The Passover

When we study the story of the Passover we are studying perhaps the most important story in the whole of the Old Testament. Jesus of Nazareth was crucified at the Feast of Passover. The meaning of the death of Jesus is given by these events in Exodus 11 and 12. The New Testament has no new explanation for the death of Jesus the Christ. It simply refers us back to what happened in these chapters of Exodus.

---

[4] See the Book-by-Book study guide on Genesis for more analysis of Genesis 22.

When these events happened between Moses and Pharaoh long ago, it was the death of Jesus of Nazareth that was intended all along. Remember Luke 22 at the Last Supper – the Passover supper – the bread and wine were there, but what about the Lamb? It was Jesus Himself who was the Passover Lamb, arrested later that very evening.

When the Angel of the LORD came in divine anger with fatal judgement against Egypt's firstborn, He knew that He would one day be the victim of that same divine anger as the firstborn who would bear the judgement of the whole world. There was nothing easy or dispassionate about that night of judgement and wrath for the Angel of the LORD.

c. The Night of the Passover (Exodus 12:1-51)

On the night of the Passover, the LORD instructs each Israelite household to kill a lamb and place its blood on the door-frame of the house. Why? How could this blood help the household on the night of judgement? Exodus 12:12-13: it was the Festival of Passover because the LORD would 'pass over' any house marked with the blood of a freshly killed lamb. Only a death could avert death. The destroying Angel was turned aside from the blood-stained house because judgment had already fallen there and the sprinkled blood was the memorial of that death.

"Not one of you shall go out the door of his house until morning", verse 22.

What sobering words. The Angel of the LORD could provide no safety for even the Israelites if they did not shelter under the lamb's shed blood. There was no place of safety for anyone other than the lamb's blood.

This is a wonderful picture of our salvation through the blood of Jesus Christ, our Passover Lamb, slaughtered on the cross. It is the blood of the Lamb of God that will cause the judgement of God to pass over us on the future day of His wrath.

When He sees the blood, He will pass over us.

The Passover meal had to be repeated every year as an annual statement of faith in the cross of the Promised Messiah – right until the day of the Last Supper when a new meal of the Cross would be installed. What a great testimony to the cross of Christ!

> Come, let us keep the Passover this night, and think of the night when the Lord delivered us out of Egypt. Let us behold our Saviour Jesus as the Paschal Lamb on which we feed; yea, let us not only look at him as such, but let us sit down to-night at his table, let us eat of his flesh and drink of his blood; for his flesh is meat indeed, and his blood is drink indeed. In holy solemnity let our hearts approach that ancient supper; let us go back to Egypt's darkness, and by holy contemplation behold, instead of the destroying angel, the angel of the covenant, at the head of the feast,-"the Lamb of God which taketh away the sins of the world."[5]

Can we imagine Nadab, Aaron's eldest son, the next morning? He wakes, hears the screams of those who have lost loved ones, and sees the bones of the lamb which was killed in his household the night before. As he looks at the lamb, he thinks – "that lamb died for me".

Exodus 12:48-49, "The same law applies to the native-born and to the alien living among you."

The Passover was a time of evangelism, a time when *Gentiles* could be welcomed in and celebrate the Passover meal on equal terms with a native-born. Israel was never a merely genetically defined nation – and we should always reject any attempts to speak of it as if it were.

The Passover theology – that redemption takes place as the Lamb is killed and His blood applied – would be kept in the very front of the Church's thinking until the Lamb of God actually died. When modern religious people try to reject this bloody theology of substitution, they simply reveal their ignorance of these basic theological events and teachings.

Spurgeon wrote:

> "It is blood, blood, blood, blood! that saves. It is not blood mixed with the water of our poor works; it is blood, blood, blood, blood! and nothing else. And the only way of salvation is by blood. For, without the shedding of blood there is no remission of sin."

---

[5] C. H. Spurgeon, Christ our Passover, preached December 2nd 1855

d. Leading His people (Exodus 13:1-22)

In Etham, 13:20-22, Moses shows us that the Angel of the LORD had been leading the whole exodus. Look at verses 17-18. The Angel of God led them through the safest route out of Egypt, even though it took longer. He did this so that they would not be discouraged by any conflict. He obviously loves and cares for His people and is not indifferent to our weaknesses.

The pillar of cloud and the pillar of fire marked out the presence of the Angel of God among the Israelites. It was like a mighty neon sign pointing down out of the heavens saying, "here He is!"

These pillars were a constant feature of the life of the church in the wilderness, pillars that would be represented within the Tabernacle itself.

The pillar of fire constantly indicated the meeting of heaven and earth in the Person of the Angel of the LORD.

Study 4   Bible Study Questions

Exodus 12:29-42

Coming out of Egypt on the night of the Passover was to be an event which was celebrated yearly by the Israelites, to remember the LORD's salvation of His people.

1. Verses 29-30: Look at the way in which the Angel of the LORD treats the Egyptians compared to His own people. Why does He make this distinction? Could the Egyptians have avoided this terrible plague or were they condemned because of their nationality? (see 12:48-49)

2. Verses 33-34: In the previous chapter, the LORD had instructed the Israelites to eat bread made without yeast. Why was this important? What might it signify if the Israelites had stayed to put yeast in their bread?

3. The Passover festival was observed yearly from that day and the Israelites were never to eat bread made with yeast during that time. If we were observing this feast, how do you think it would make us think about our present life on earth when eating the unleavened bread? What would it help us to keep our eyes fixed on?

4. Verses 35-36: How did these Hebrew slaves manage to take so many riches from Egypt as they set out as refugees? What will these riches be used for? (see 25:1-9 but also 32:2-4)

5. How can knowing this help us trust the Lord for times in our own lives when we are in need? What warning is there in the 32:2-4 passage for how we use the things the Lord has provided for us?

6. Verses 37-39: Look at the mixture of people that came up out of Egypt at the Exodus. If this event is a picture of the way the LORD brings His people out of sin, why is it important that each of these are mentioned? (a) men and women; (b) children; (c) many other people; (d) many animals.

7. Verses 40-42: This takes us back to Genesis 15:12-16. We need to think about what the Israelites must have thought after so many years in Egypt. Did they still trust the prophecy or did they assume that the Word of the LORD had forgotten?

Study 4   Further Questions

1. Why did the ancient Church need to remember this night of Passover every single year? In the light of Genesis 22:8 and 20, what kind of conversations must have taken place among the faithful families each year as they ate the roast lamb?

2. The explanation of 'bread without yeast' is given in Exodus 12:39. Those that wanted to wait for their bread to rise in Egypt were choosing fluffy bread over their redemption! What does this tell us about the Feast of Yeast-free (Unleavened) Bread? Can you find more of the references to bread-without-yeast in the Bible? Can you see how each of them teaches the same lesson about redemption?

Study 4   Daily Readings

Day 1	Exodus 11
Day 2	Exodus 12
Day 3	Exodus 13
Day 4	Luke 22:7-38
Day 5	Isaiah 53
Day 6	2 Chronicles 35:1-19
Day 7	Revelation 5

The daily Bible readings are an opportunity not only to read through all of the material in the book under study, but also to read parts of the Bible that relate to the themes and issues that we have been considering. We try to make sure that we receive light from the whole Bible as we think through the key issues each week.

The Red Sea

Study 5   The LORD delivers

Exodus 14-18

> **Key Truth:** The Angel of the LORD protects and sustains His people through all hardships.

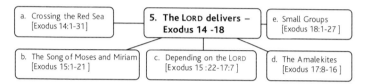

a.   Crossing the Red Sea (Exodus 14:1-31)

Pharaoh stirs up an insane hue and cry after Israel. He gathered the very best of his armies to persecute the Church. The Angel of the LORD uses this as an opportunity to present His redeeming power clearly to the world. Sin is revealed in its horror once more.

Moses preferred the shame of Christ to the luxuries of Egypt (Hebrews 11:25-26), but we can see in 14:10-12 that this did not apply to most of the Israelites.

Exodus 14:14 is a marvellous memory verse.

> The LORD will fight for you; you need only to be still.

It is a wonderful description of how the LORD saves – justification by faith alone in Christ alone. They did not need to fear – only trust in the Angel of the LORD who was redeeming them.

In verses 19-20 we are shown that the cloud was not the same thing as the LORD Himself. Some people have simply assumed that the LORD appeared *in the form of a cloud* or that the Angel of the LORD was identical with the cloud. But this does not seem to be so – the LORD traveled *within* the cloud, and in these verses He walks through the Israelite camp to stand behind them, protecting them from the persecutors.

It is important for us to realise who is the true Leader and Redeemer of Israel. Moses was unique in Israel, standing between the Angel of the

Lord and the people. Moses was the appointed leader and, as we see in both Exodus and Numbers, the way people viewed Moses was their view of the Lord Himself – see, for example, Numbers 16.

However, the Mediator between God and humanity is not and never was Moses. There has only ever been one Mediator between God and humanity and that is the Angel of the Lord, the One who later became one of us, born of the Virgin Mary, the man Christ Jesus – see 1 Timothy 2:5.

The mighty *Spirit* (NIV 'wind') of the Lord came to drive back the Red Sea and open a way across for the Israelites.

To display such mastery over the sea glorifies the Angel of the Lord. This is not just like any other miracle. It is an extreme example of the absolute power of the Living God to do exactly as He pleases. Throughout the Bible the sea is a symbol of chaos and lawlessness. If the Holy Spirit can overpower even the unruly and rebellious sea, then there is nothing that He cannot do.

On seeing that, what would the Egyptians do? The power of the Lord Christ[6] to do everything that He promised had been miraculously demonstrated before their eyes so many times. Surely, now would be the moment to repent. Yet, human sin and unbelief is utter madness. There is nothing reasonable about resisting Jesus Christ. There is nothing to be admired or respected about refusing the Gospel of God.

The Egyptian army of Exodus 14 stands as a testimony down through history warning the whole world of the inevitable fate of those who will not trust in Jesus Christ.

In verse 31 we see that it was a time when many of the Israelites became believers in the Angel of the Lord.

b. The Song of Moses and Miriam (Exodus 15:1-21)

Picture the scene at the end of Exodus 14. The bodies of thousands of men and animals floating in the water – many others washed up on the

---

[6] I was once asked whether people in the Old Testament knew that their Lord was the Messiah. Perhaps they thought the Messiah was just a created human like them! However, in Lamentations 4:20 in the original Hebrew and in the Greek translation the Messiah is called the Lord. In most English translations it is wrongly translated 'the Lord's anointed' rather than "the Messiah is the Lord" or 'the Anointed Lord' or 'the Messiah Lord'.

shoreline. News begins to filter out – no survivors. At the same time, on the opposite side of the water, a huge gathering of maybe 3 million people. They can see some of the bodies washed up on the shore.

Suddenly, the leader of this vast church gathering sings a prayer to the Lord God. It is not a prayer for the bereaved families. Nor is it in anyway sad about what has happened.

Many find this kind of incident in the Old Testament a little difficult. One of the most common objections raised against the Bible centres on the way such violent deaths are given such divine approval.

However, we must remember how incredibly patient the Lord had been. The terrible judgement of chapter 15 had not come without warning. Over and over again the Lord sent Moses to Pharaoh with more and more opportunities for repentance. Yet, on each occasion the Gospel had been rejected. The Angel of the Lord had sent Moses to that ancient unbelieving empire many times. The church had even lived amongst them for more than 400 years – but many did not fear the Word of the Lord.

It is against this background that we must study Moses' and Miriam's prayer of praise in Exodus chapter 15.

Through the Red Sea victory, the Lord Christ had just given a limited presentation of the final judgement at His Second Coming. The people who trusted Him were saved and those that refused Him were judged. It was such a vivid moment of Gospel truth that Moses could do nothing other than sing this mighty prayer of praise.

Exodus 15 challenges us to pray with greater praise – to fill our prayers with accounts of the mighty victories of the Lord over evil.

c. Depending on the Lord (Exodus 15:22-17:7)

The people of God were utterly dependent on the grace of God in the Mediator. They were in a humanly impossible position. For millions of people (plus livestock) to go into a desert would mean death by thirst or starvation.

When the Church crossed the Red Sea it went from pagan slavery into sheer dependence on the Lord.

This was a key experience for them. It was a time of testing and learning. The Angel of the Lord promised that they would enjoy some of the blessings of the New Creation (freedom from disease), if they obeyed Him – 15:25-26. This should have established them in total confidence in the care and providence of their LORD forever. However, they didn't trust Him to do this, 16:1-3.

Much worse than complaining about their food, they wished they had never trusted in the LORD in the first place. They wished that they had died in the captivity of Egypt. Contrast this with Moses' own attitude in Hebrews 11:26.

The issue was not whether they were a bit hungry or thirsty, but whether they appreciated the fellowship that they had with the LORD. How scandalous for the Church to be wishing that they had pagan luxuries when their Saviour was right there leading them and caring for them!

Grumbling particularly annoys the LORD – but on this occasion He uses it as an opportunity to preach the truth to them. Rather than providing only earthly food (like the quail) He provides them some special bread from heaven called "manna" – and in verse 11 He says that when they eat this meat and bread they will know Him to be YAHWEH their God.

The Angel of the LORD was providing them with this food as a offer of table fellowship with Him – an offer of union with Him. He was asking that they see the spiritual reality that this food represented, that they trust in Him and know Him. This is the Gospel – and the same offer is made to the Church today.

When we eat the bread and drink the wine in our Communion services it is vital that we feed on the Body and Blood of Jesus Christ rather than merely bread and wine. The words in the Church of England prayer book are so helpful: "Take and eat this in remembrance that Christ died for thee, and feed on *him* in thy heart by faith with thanksgiving."

Bread from heaven, meat from the skies and water from the rock – what miraculous provision the Angel of the LORD provided for them... and what a wonderful invitation to fellowship with *Him*!

Let this direct us to live in a dependence:

1. Upon God's providence, even in the greatest straits and difficulties. God can open fountains for our supply where we least expect them, waters in the wilderness (Isaiah 53:20), because he makes a way in the wilderness, verse 19. Those who, in this wilderness, keep to God's way, may trust him to provide for them. While we follow the pillar of cloud and fire, surely goodness and mercy shall follow us, like the water out of the rock.

2. Upon Christ's grace: *That rock was Christ,* 1 Corinthians 10:4. The graces and comforts of the Spirit are compared to rivers of living water, John 7:38, 39; 4:14. These flow from Christ, who is the rock smitten by the law of Moses, for he was made under the law. Nothing will supply the needs, and satisfy the desires, of a soul, but water out of this rock, this fountain opened. The pleasures of sense are puddle-water; spiritual delights are rock-water, so pure, so clear, so refreshing-rivers of pleasure.[7]

d. The Amalekites (Exodus 17:8-16)

The defeat of the Amalekites is another great incident from Exodus 17. The enemies can be defeated only as long as Moses stands on a hill with his arms outstretched holding the wooden staff of God. It is a man called Jesus (Joshua/Yeshua is the same name in the Hebrew) that conquers the Amalekites. As long as Moses standing with his arms held out was kept in view, Israel kept winning. It is clear why this story has attracted the attention of so many Christians preachers down the centuries.

This battle was to become a key feature in the history of Israel, Deut 25:17-19.

The Deuteronomy passage is important because it helps us to appreciate just how bad the attack of the Amalekites was. The Israelites were very thirsty, tired and on the move and the Amalekites seemed to have attacked the rear of the Israelite procession, killing all the weakest and weariest of the Israelites first of all. It was an act of total brutality and cruelty because "they had no fear of God".

These descendants of Abraham (Amalek was Esau's grandson) were completely godless. It is clearly not enough to be merely a genetic descendant of Abraham. The true children of Abraham are his spiritual children, regardless of their genetic heritage.

---

[7] Matthew Henry Commentary on the Whole Bible, Exodus 17.

e. Small Groups (Exodus 18:1-27)

Organising the Church into small groups is not a modern invention.

It was pioneered by Moses' father-in-law. One man cannot have all the charismatic gifts for the whole Church family. The church was organised into groups of ten so that everybody could have the pastoral care necessary – which means there must have been about 300,000 'fellowship groups' all together.

Imagine trying to organise all that! The descriptions of the group leaders in 18:21 is so similar to the New Testament descriptions found in 1 Timothy 3:1-7 and Titus 1:7-9.

It seems clear that Paul got his pattern from Moses.

Study 5   Bible Study Questions

Exodus 16:1-18

It has been 6 weeks since the Israelites left Egypt. They have seen the LORD's victory over their enemies in the parting of the Red Sea, and witnessed the bitter waters of Marah miraculously turn sweet for them to drink.

1. Verses 1-3: What is so bad about a starving people grumbling for food? (Psalm 78:17-22)

2. Verses 4-5: What do we learn about the LORD from His response to their wickedness?

3. What is the test the LORD is interested in? Is it a good thing or a frightening thing? What was it to lead to? Look at Deuteronomy 8 verse 2 and verse 16.

4. Verses 6-8: What was the point of the Manna from heaven? Deuteronomy 8:3. Why do you think they could not keep any until the next day, but had to gather it again in the morning? How does this help us see the way the LORD wants us to be in our relationship with Him?

5. John 6:32-35 & 48-51: What does Jesus mean when He says He is the bread from heaven?

6. How is Exodus 16 related to what Jesus said in John 6? What is the point of it for us today? 1 Corinthians 10:6, 11-12.

Study 5   Further Questions

1. Make a list of all the actions accomplished by the Angel of the LORD so far in Exodus. How should this determine our understanding of the book?

2. The Old Testament has many stories in which many people are killed either directly from the LORD or by His command. These events challenge us and disturb us. We might want to avoid such stories, ignore them, explain them away or even deny them completely. However, in the light of the coming Day of God, what do we need to learn from such events? If a world leader today tried to use these passages to justify their own violence, what would we say? Are these stories about any nation or just ancient Israel?

Study 5   Daily Readings

Day 1	Exodus 14
Day 2	Exodus 15
Day 3	Exodus 16
Day 4	Exodus 17
Day 5	Exodus 18
Day 6	Psalm 106
Day 7	John 6:25-60

The daily Bible readings are an opportunity not only to read through all of the material in the book under study, but also to read parts of the Bible that relate to the themes and issues that we have been considering. We try to make sure that we receive light from the whole Bible as we think through the key issues each week.

Led by the Lord

Study 6   The LORD speaks

Exodus 19-24

> **Key Truth:** Living a holy life is built on salvation by grace through faith in the Messiah.

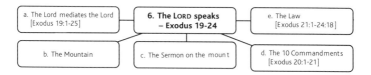

a.   The LORD mediates the LORD (Exodus 19:1-25)

It has taken the children of Israel 2 months to arrive at Mount Sinai from the day of the Exodus, but chapters 19 to 24 cover a period of 3 days.

What happened in this short time at Mount Sinai is spoken about in the rest of the Bible with great reverence. Just look at what Moses says about this event in Deuteronomy 4:32: "Has anything so great as this ever happened, or has anything like it ever been heard of?"

What is the big deal? Why is it a unique event?

Why is Exodus 19 viewed with such awe and wonder?

Throughout Genesis and Exodus up to this point, the LORD appeared to people and He spoke to them in face to face conversations.

Some examples of this happening are:

- Genesis 12:7
- Genesis 8:1
- Genesis 26:24
- Genesis 35:7-9
- Exodus 3:2
- Exodus 4:5.
- Genesis 17:1
- Genesis 26:2
- Genesis 35:1
- Genesis 48:3
- Exodus 3:16

However, something quite different happened at Mount Sinai. According to Deuteronomy 4:15 *no form of any kind was seen when the LORD spoke out of the fire*. What was happening here? Why this sudden change in the way the Lord interacted with His people?

In Exodus 19:3 Moses went up the mountain to God. The LORD reminds Moses of what He (the Angel of the LORD) had done for them in getting them out of Egypt. He now wants them to be a nation of priests – a nation who shows Him to the world and brings the world to Him. When the people agree to this, 19:8, Moses returns up the mountain to God.

From verse 10 the conversation takes a strange turn. Moses is meeting with *God* on the mountain, but God says to him – "be ready by the third day, because on that day *the LORD* will come down on Mount Sinai…"

God is already on the mountain, so who else is going to arrive? The mountain is to be put off limits (verses 12-13) and only when the ram's horn sounded could all the people go up the mountain.

So, the *Lord* on the mountain tells Moses and the people to get ready for the *Lord* to come down onto the mountain.[8]

In verse 18 the LORD descended onto the mountain, and in verse 20 there is another descent of the LORD to the top of the mountain.

Moses is summoned up and someone called the LORD tells him to "warn the people so they do not force their way through to see the LORD… or the LORD will break out against them." Notice that the LORD does not say "I will break out against them."

What is happening here, with two Lords on Mount Sinai?

The Angel of the LORD has brought His people to meet with *the LORD* – the Son has brought His people to the Father.

---

[8] When we think about God the Father coming from heaven to earth, being located in one place rather than another, we must be careful not to overstate this. The Living God fills the whole universe. The Father, Son and Holy Spirit live a life so infinitely beyond all created existence. Nevertheless, within the Bible it is clear that the Father and the Son do uniquely manifest their presence in particular places. Thus, we may speak of the Father enthroned in heaven and the Son sitting at His right hand.

The Angel of the Lord has brought the church out of slavery, has provided for them daily and has now led them to the place where the Father has chosen to speak from heaven. What a wonderful thing! How privileged this ancient church was to be in this position. Although they would not see Him, yet they would hear the actual voice of the Father speaking to them from heaven, telling them how they should live. No wonder Moses wrote Deut 4:32!

Perhaps one of the clearest explanations of this is to be read in the words of Philo, a Jewish theologian who was born c. 30 BC, before the New Testament was written.

He recognised that the One God was more then one person, more than one LORD. He explained that one LORD spoke face to face with Moses, standing between Moses and another LORD whose face could not be seen. His comment on Deut 5:5 is as follows:

> The Father has given the Word, his eldest and chief messenger, the special privilege of standing at the border separating what has been made from the Maker. On the one hand, he is ever before the Incorruptible (God) as intercessor for the perishing mortal and on the other, he is the ambassador of the Head to the subject. He rejoices in the privilege and magnifies it in detail by saying: 'I stood between the Lord and you'...

b. The Mountain

In Deuteronomy 4:36 and Nehemiah 9:13, we are told that the Lord actually spoke *from heaven* at the time when He spoke to Moses on the top of Mount Sinai. It is as if Mount Sinai and heaven itself are joined together at the top of the mountain, as if Moses could enter into heaven by going up the mountain. It was on this mountain that the Lord gave instructions for the Tabernacle to be built. Therefore, Hebrews 8:5 seems to confirm that Moses saw the *heavenly realities* that the Tabernacle was a copy of.

The mountain was covered in fire. As we have learned in previous studies, we see that there is a barrier of fire between heaven and earth. Mount Sinai stands at the boundary of heaven and earth.

We remember, too, that the people were waiting for a ram's horn to be blown (19:13) before going up the mountain to meet the Lord.

However, look what happened when the trumpet was sounded. The people were too afraid to believe the words of the Lord and refused to go up the mountain to where the Unseen Lord was. Instead, they stayed at a distance and sent Moses up alone.

What a sinful tragedy! The goal of our salvation is to approach the Father, and yet the ancient church refused that unique experience of it.

c. The Sermon on the Mount

Exodus 21 begins the original Sermon on the Mount.

The Unseen Lord spoke from within the thick darkness, from heaven. The only time when the voice of the Father is heard like this again is three times during the earthly life of Jesus (Luke 3:22 and 9:35, and John 12:28-29). This is a truly remarkable moment in the Bible. The giving of the Law is a solemn and majestic moment.

The first words of the Invisible God[9] from heaven to the people redeemed by His Divine Angel, are words of grace, not demand. "I am the LORD your God, who brought you out of Egypt, out of the land of slavery."

The words are not 'this is what you must do', but 'this is what I have done'.

He shows us through this that the Gospel message is about faith in what the Lord has done for His people, not what we can do for Him.

In the light of what He has done for them, the Lord goes on to describe how they are now able to live, as an expression of their gratitude and the new life they have through faith in their LORD.

---

[9] The Father's title in Colossians 1:15 is 'the invisible God' and it seems the right title to use for Him during this time when He was hidden in the thick darkness in Exodus.

d. The 10 Commandments (Exodus 20:1-21)

It is important for us to appreciate just what these ten commandments are. They are such a deeply treasured part of the Bible. Generations of the Church have committed them to memory and they have formed the basic guidebook to Christian living for millions and millions of the saints.

Sometimes the 10 commandments are seen as general rules given to humanity quite separate from the good news about the Messiah. They are almost seen as 'what God wants from us even if we don't believe in the Messiah'!

However, the more we study them the more we see that they have no meaning without the Messiah and His salvation. The constant theme is that the LORD is the God of the people who are spoken to.

This is not abstract moral law, but gracious instructions to Gospel-people.

The first commandment is built on the fact that the people have experienced redemption.

The second commandment assumes that the LORD is their God and that He is jealous of their love and faith.

The third commandment not only assumes that they know that His Name is 'The LORD' or 'YAHWEH', but that they know how to treat this Name properly.

The fourth commandment is not simply about 'having a day off', but keeping a day holy 'to the LORD'.

The fifth commandment is locked into the promise of 'the land'. The fathers and mothers must teach their children about trusting in the LORD so that they will inherit the Promised Land and eternal life.

Commandments six to nine are the ones that non-Christians like to talk about, but when we remember how Jesus explained them in Matthew 5 we see that they are also part of Kingdom living rather than mere civic morality.

The tenth commandment examines the heart expecting us to be content with the LORD's provision for us.

As we learn and treasure these precious words of Scripture, we must constantly relate them to the ways of Jesus. God the Son is the perfect expression of the Law of God, and all the Law of God is aimed at describing the ways and works of our Divine Messiah.

e. The Law (Exodus 21:1-24:18)

This Sermon on the Mount is preached to describe what it means in practical terms for the Israelites to live as citizens of the Kingdom of God. It is addressed to those who already have been redeemed.

This is what it looks like to live as the redeemed Church of God.

The laws reflect how the grace of God is to make an impact on *every* aspect of life. It is a holistic description of kingdom living, of living between the times. In each case we are shown how Gospel grace transforms situations.

Whether it is dealing with economic debts (21:1-11) or personal injuries (21:12-36) there is a determination to overturn the attitudes and practices of the pagan world and replace them with the ways of justice and freedom. If we read property laws of 22:1-15, we can see how justice and integrity run through them.

The heart of the Living God can be heard beating through 22:16-23:9. There is no room for behaviour that attacks the heart of this Almighty and Holy God... and yet the cry of the widow or orphan is always heard (22:22-23).

Do not follow the crowd in doing wrong – 23:2

These are words that hit home to us today as forcefully as when they were first spoken. These laws apply that truth to the culture and context of the ancient church but we musty be spiritually alive to apply them to our own culture and context. Where do we fall into immorality or ignore injustice? If these laws are written on our hearts we must find the ways of justice, love and truth that pour from the Living God.

The laws concerning Sabbaths and festivals (23:10-19) are full of spiritual treasure. Spend time considering what aspects of the Messiah are shown by these laws. Consider 23:20-33 as the Angel of the LORD goes ahead of them to prepare their Promised Land. Think how this throws light on the meaning of those festivals.

Finally, when this brief introductory summary of the laws of God had been given, we arrive at glorious wonder and mystery that is Exodus chapter 24. We have saved this chapter for special consideration in the Bible study.

| Study 6 | Bible Study Questions |

Exodus 24:1-18

The Bible is full of wonderful events, and there are few that can match the fellowship meal of Exodus 24. It is a passage that gives us an exciting insight into the heart of the Living Trinitarian God.

1. Verses 1-2: Who is this that the elders are going to *see*? (remember John 1:18)

2. Verses 3-4: The Israelites vow to keep the laws, yet what happens the very next time we see the Israelites (Chapter 32)? Which laws from chapter 20 did they break?

3. Verses 5-8: What is the importance of the blood and the sacrifices? What does it do here? What does it remind us of?

4. Verses 9-11: What can we learn about the Lord from this incident?

5. Why didn't seeing the Lord make these elders more obedient to Him? How did the people who saw the Son after His human birth react to Him?

6. Verses 12-13: Joshua went on to lead Israel mightily. What can we learn from this story and the following verses about the way in which he grew to become the next leader of the Israelites? See also Exodus 33:9-11 and Numbers 14:6-9.

7. What can we learn about our own Christian living and service from studying Joshua?

8. Verses 14-18: What is happening in these verses? What can you imagine the watching Israelites must have felt at this time? How did they understand God to be?

Study 6   Further Questions

1.   Most of our speech and writing about the Trinity today is dominated by just one set of their titles – 'the Father', 'the Son' and 'the Holy Spirit'. As we study Exodus, and the rest of the Hebrew Scriptures, we find many more titles for the Divine Persons. We have become familiar with the title 'Angel of the LORD' for the Son and we can see why the Father is also called the Most High or the Invisible God. Should we use a wider range of the Bible's titles for the Persons? What effect might this have on our Bible reading?

2.   Where else in the Bible do we hear the ram's horn being blown? (Joshua 6, Leviticus 25:9) Why was the ram's horn blown on those occasions?

Study 6   Daily Readings

Day 1	Exodus 19
Day 2	Exodus 20
Day 3	Exodus 21
Day 4	Exodus 22
Day 5	Exodus 23
Day 6	Exodus 24
Day 7	Matthew 5

The daily Bible readings are an opportunity not only to read through all of the material in the book under study, but also to read parts of the Bible that relate to the themes and issues that we have been considering. We try to make sure that we receive light from the whole Bible as we think through the key issues each week.

The Golden Calf

Study 7   The LORD mediates

Exodus 32-34

Key Truth: The true God of Israel is Father, Son and Holy Spirit.

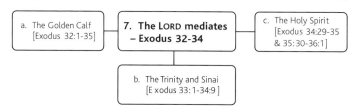

a. The Golden Calf
[Exodus 32:1-35]

7. The LORD mediates – Exodus 32-34

c. The Holy Spirit
[Exodus 34:29-35 & 35:30-36:1]

b. The Trinity and Sinai
[Exodus 33:1-34:9]

a.   The Golden Calf (Exodus 32:1-35)

When we get to the end of chapter 31 we are not expecting things to go so horribly wrong.

We have just witnessed Mount Sinai enveloped in fire as the Invisible God, the Father, descended on top of the mountain to meet with His people and give them instructions to live holy lives. The Angel of the Lord has led them to this place, miraculously delivering and providing for them along the way. We are shocked when we reach chapter 32 and discover the Israelites making and worshipping a golden calf.

How could the people so quickly forget the love and redemption of the Living God?

At one level we can look back with shocked disbelief at the ingratitude and wilful disobedience of those ancient "people of God". Yet we need to be careful. If we know our own hearts we know that we are capable of the same sinfulness. All too often we forget the kindness of our God and follow our selfish, evil desires.

Instead of self-righteously looking back, let's fall to our knees and beg that our Heavenly Father would "deliver us from evil and lead us not into temptation".

This incident comes sandwiched between the instructions for the tabernacle and the building of the tabernacle, and we are meant to notice this.

The Israelites use the gold that they plundered from idolaters of Egypt and channel it back into idolatry.

This gold was provided by the Lord for the building of His Tabernacle. The Israelites (verse 4) built the golden calf as their own "visible form of the Invisible God" (compare Colossians 1:15). However, now the Lord in His kindness is going to teach them that there is only One Mediator – One visible form of the Invisible God.

Why do they worship a golden *calf*? What is significant about a cow or bull?

It is true that the Hindus regard the cow as a sacred animal, and we find the same reverence for the bull in many ancient cultures.

Perhaps the best explanation for this actually comes in Ezekiel chapters 1 and 10. In Ezekiel 1:10 we see that the spiritual creatures have four faces: a lion, eagle, man and *bull*. In Ezekiel chapter 10:14 the four faces are described again and this time they are a lion, eagle, man and *cherub*. This implies that the face of a bull is the same as the face of a cherub. Perhaps this helps us to understand how the truth could become corrupted into the strange bull-worshipping religions around the world.

Perhaps we could go even further. In Ezekiel 28 there is a description of one particular cherub – the guardian cherub of Eden, Satan himself. If Satan is a cherub, then is it possible that in one sense the worship of the golden calf was a form of Satan worship? This would certainly help us to understand why the Lord and Moses reacted with such anger.

To understand the death of the *3000* people by the sword of the Levites (32:28), we need to understand that this is the *50th* day after leaving Egypt. In the New Testament, *50* days after Jesus' victory over sin at the cross, the Lord once again shook the earth. He sent fire and the mighty Spirit on the day of Pentecost (meaning "the 50th day"). On this day, instead of giving an external proclamation of the Gospel as He did at Sinai, God gave the reality to which the Law always pointed – salvation in the Spirit. In Acts 2:41 we read that "those who accepted his message were baptised, and *3000* were added to their number that day". It seems as if the two '50th day' events reflect each other, one in judgement and the other in salvation.

b. The Trinity and Sinai (Exodus 33:1-34:9)

Exodus 33-35 includes a fascinating presentation of the Trinity. It is worth studying it carefully because it can help the outsider to see that 'the doctrine of the Trinity' is not an abstract theory, but a description of the life and work of the God of Scripture.

In Exodus 33 during the giving of the Law, Moses is at Mount Sinai meeting with the Living God. He would go up to the top of the mountain to meet with a person called the LORD, Yahweh, who was hidden from Moses' sight in thick darkness. As we have previously studied, in Deuteronomy 4:12 Moses recalls that although the voice of this Yahweh-Person was heard, yet 'no form' was seen. The Yahweh-Person in the thick darkness is never seen. However, that is not the only person called Yahweh, the LORD, that Moses would meet with.

In Exodus 33:7-11 Moses explains how he used to meet with the LORD *face to face* as a man speaks to his friend in a tent pitched at the bottom of the mountain.

> "The LORD would speak to Moses face to face, as a man speaks with his friend."

THIS Yahweh-Person had already been seen. A description of one such time is Exodus 24:9-11.

Moses goes to speak to the unseen LORD who meets with him on top of the mountain. The people of Israel had been unfaithful to the LORD and Moses wants the Presence of the LORD to go with them to show that He still accepts them.

However, Moses wants something even more – he wants to see this hidden LORD. He wants Him to take away this thick darkness so that Moses can see His face.

He is not content with seeing the visible Lord, but asks for more… he wants to see the Invisible God.

However, the Unseen LORD of the thick darkness cannot do this. He is prepared to tell Moses His Name, to describe His character to Moses, but He cannot show him His face – verse 20 & 23.

> "You cannot see my face, for no-one may see me and live."
> "My face must not be seen".

When the Unseen LORD speaks His name to Moses, then Moses realises that the character and reality of the Unseen LORD had already been fully shown to Him in the Angel of the Lord. This is why Moses reacts in the way he does in Exodus 34:8-9, asking for forgiveness – "O Lord, let the Lord go with us."

The great hymn writer Augustus Montague Toplady (1740-1778) wrote his famous hymn all about Moses hiding in the cleft of a rock (Exodus 33:22):

> Rock of Ages, cleft for me,
> Let me hide myself in Thee;
> Let the water and the blood
> From Thy riven side which flowed
> Be of sin the double cure,
> Cleanse me from its guilt and power.

The picture of Moses hiding in the Rock of Christ as the only way of contact with the Father is a clear image of our relationship with the Father. We are His sons and daughters because we are hidden in Christ, the eternal Son of God.

It is vital for us to be able to explain the truth of the Trinity. Too often people have described our God as an impossible puzzle or an endless mathematical enigma. However, the more we study the life and actions of the Three Persons, the more we will understand them.

Rather than treating them as a riddle to be solved, we must watch in joy and worship as their life makes sense of our lives, as their relationship with each other unravels the deepest issues of life.

c. The Holy Spirit (Exodus 34:29-35 & 35:30-36:1)

There is a third Person called the LORD – and we see Him in Exodus 35.

The Israelites had been instructed to make a special tent for the LORD to live in as He travelled with them – but making this tent was a very difficult job. So, another Person called the LORD, the Spirit of God, comes to live in those craftsmen who have this job in order to empower them with skill, ability and knowledge for this task, 35:30-33.

We need to be careful if we speak of "the *coming* of the Holy Spirit on the day of Pentecost". It is true that on that day in Acts 2 the Spirit was poured out on all flesh as never before…but we should not think that the Holy Spirit only began to work on the day of Pentecost. He was at work filling and equipping the saints from the beginning of the world!

The Spirit equips the Church to accomplish her mission. This has always been the work of the Spirit and it still is today as He gives us all various charismatic gifts.

This is the way in which the Living God always works throughout the Bible. *From the Father (the Unseen Lord), through the Son (the Seen Lord) by the power of the Spirit.* Exodus chapters 33-35 is perhaps the best part of the Bible to see all three Persons of the Trinity, and the way they interact with each other and with the Church.

Study 7   Bible Study Questions

Exodus 32:1-25

The worship of the golden calf is one of the darkest moments in the Hebrew Scriptures. Instead of looking down on such evil, we need to be warned and see the danger in our own lives.

1.   Verse 1: Why did the people want to make an idol to worship? Why do you think they requested 'gods' not 'a god'?

2.   Verses 2-6: What should Aaron's response have been? How far is he a victim of the people here?

3.   Look at how God said the people should be behaving during this time – 20:20-25. How many direct contradictions can you see with how they actually behaved?

4.   Verses 7-10: What do we learn about the Lord from His reaction to this people's idolatry?

5.   Verses 11-14: How does Moses' reply to the Lord? Why doesn't he just agree with Him? What can we learn about prayer from this incident?

6.   Verses 21-24: Look at Aaron's responses when Moses accuses him. What does this tell us about sin? Given that the LORD already knew what happened, why does Aaron make such empty excuses?

7.   Verse 25: What effect did the sin of the Israelites have on their evangelistic outreach? How should this encourage us to live?

Study 7   Further Questions

1. If a Muslim neighbour challenges us to explain the Trinity, how would we do it? It is sometimes said that the Trinity is a late idea invented by Christian philosophers long after the Bible was written. What is the best answer to this?

2. Sometimes people suggest that God is not revealed as a Trinity in the Old Testament. Why do you think there has been such confusion about this?

3. If you talk to someone who sees the cow as a sacred animal, is there a way of using this as a good starting point for a spiritual conversation? Can we acknowledge the 'spiritual truth' in this whilst pointing to the real and final truth of Jesus?

Study 7   Daily Readings

Day 1	Exodus 32
Day 2	Exodus 33
Day 3	Exodus 34
Day 4	Psalm 78
Day 5	Nehemiah 9:5-37
Day 6	Colossians 1:15-23
Day 7	Deuteronomy 32:1-43

The daily Bible readings are an opportunity not only to read through all of the material in the book under study, but also to read parts of the Bible that relate to the themes and issues that we have been considering. We try to make sure that we receive light from the whole Bible as we think through the key issues each week.

The Heavenly Tabernacle

Study 8   The Layout of the tabernacle

Key Truth: The Tabernacle is a model of the relationship between heaven and earth.

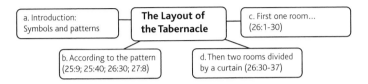

a. Introduction: Symbols and patterns

The Layout of the Tabernacle

c. First one room... (26:1-30)

b. According to the pattern (25:9; 25:40; 26:30; 27:8)

d. Then two rooms divided by a curtain (26:30-37)

a.   Introduction: Symbols and patterns

Hopefully by now we have got quite used to thinking in symbolic terms.

When we considered the Passover of Exodus chapter 12 we saw that the blood applied to the doorposts symbolised that death had already visited that household, that the judgement for sin had already been paid.

When we saw the bush burning with fire back in chapter 3 we realised that the fire symbolised the barrier between heaven and earth.

One of the most important lessons to learn in understanding all that happens in the Bible is appreciated the symbolic character of so many objects and events. The ways of the Living God have a *pattern* and this *pattern* is impressed upon so many of the objects and events in the Bible.

Whenever He brings victory through weakness, we recognise this pattern. It is so typical of the Lord God to do that! When we see the way that blood is applied to bring cleansing, we might acknowledge that it seems a strange way of cleaning things, but we also recognise that this 'logic' of cleansing is the way of the Living God. The pattern or way of the Living God is that sin can only be cleansed through the shedding of blood.

When reading the book of Genesis the writer of the book of Hebrews noted that the way that Abraham, Isaac and Jacob lived in tents showed that they saw their present life as a temporary stage in a journey to a permanent *heavenly* home (see Hebrews 11:8-16). When the animal sacrifices were offered throughout the Old Testament, it is obvious that the animal's blood could not actually atone for sin. Rather, the sacrifice of the animal was pointing to the blood of the Lamb of God, Jesus the Messiah, whose blood really can take away the sins of the world.

In the New Testament, when Jesus healed the blind man in Mark 8, we are learning not only that Jesus can heal physical blindness, but that He heals spiritual blindness. The blind man physically symbolises the *spiritual* blindness of the whole human race.

If we are to see the point of the Scriptures, we must be alive to the *implications* of all that we read. We must always ask, "why did the Holy Spirit cause this to be written? What truth did He want us to grasp through this?"

When we come to consider the tabernacle described in the book of Exodus we come to one of the most important *patterns* in the whole Bible. The rest of the Bible uses the *pattern* of the tabernacle – the layout of the rooms, the furniture, the priestly activities – to explain so many truths.

If we have understand the basic symbolism of the tabernacle we will find many parts of the Bible much easier to understand.

b.   According to the pattern (25:9; 25:40; 26:30; 27:8)

One of the first things for us to notice is that the pattern of the tabernacle is described *twice* for us in the book of Exodus: first when the Lord is describing how it should be made (Exodus 25-31); second when the tabernacle is actually made)Exodus 35-40).

If the Holy Spirit went to the trouble of recording all these details *twice* then it must be extremely important for us to understand.

At first sight it can all seem quite intimidating. For most of us reading through these 'tabernacle chapters' seems very complicated and confusing. What does it all mean? What would it have looked like?

It becomes a lot easier if we can see a picture or model of what the tabernacle would have looked like. Then the detailed instructions begin to make sense and we can see that there is an order to the description, a careful unfolding of how the building worked.

The instructions are divided into distinct sections by the Lord.

He used a particular phrase to divide or 'punctuate' the instructions. Moses went up into the thick darkness on top of the mountain (Exodus 24:15-18) and it is almost as if he were shown the reality of heaven and earth in the presence of the Unseen Lord. It is as if Moses were shown the 'workings' of heaven and earth so that he would understand the little model of reality that he was about to build.

Throughout the instructions the Lord says "Make this according to the pattern shown you on the mountain".

This repeated phrase helps us to see that the instructions are divided into distinct sections.

25:1-8	THE MATERIALS
25:9	*Make this tabernacle and all its furnishings exactly like the pattern I will show you.*
25:10-39	THE FURNITURE
25:40	*See that you make them according to the pattern shown you on the mountain.*
26:1-29	THE TABERNACLE STRUCTURE
26:30	*Set up the tabernacle according to the plan shown you on the mountain.*
26:31-27:7	THE DIVIDING CURTAIN AND THE ALTAR OF BURNT OFFERING.
27:8	*It is to be made just as you were shown on the mountain.*
27:9-31:10	THE PRIESTLY WORK OF THE TABERNACLE
31:11	*They are to make them just as I commanded you.*

c. First one room... (26:1-30)

Although the tabernacle furniture is the first section of the instructions we will examine that furniture in more detail in the next chapter.

In order to help us understand the significance of that furniture, we begin with the basic tabernacle structure given in Exodus chapter 26.

The first time that a person reads this chapter it can seem an overwhelming amount of detail, yet it is actually describing a fairly simple room.

The measurements are in 'cubits'. A cubit is an ancient standard of measurement based on the distance from the elbow to the tip of the fingers. Although this may vary from person to person, yet it gives us a figure of roughly 18 inches or 45cm.

The tabernacle was constructed of frames that were 1.5 cubits wide and 10 cubits long (Exodus 26:15-16).

There were 20 of these frames forming each of the two long sides (Exodus 26:18-21). The end wall was formed by 6 of the frames, with special corner pieces to make it a total of 10 cubits wide (Exodus 26:22-25).

Therefore, the tabernacle was a covered wooden structure measuring 45 feet long, 15 feet wide and 15 feet high – or 13.5 metres long, 4.5 metres wide and 4.5 metres high.

As the tabernacle is described in the first section (Exodus 26:1-29) it is a single, undivided room.

This is tremendously important. As we will see, the tabernacle structure represents the heaven and the earth. Later we will see that a curtain was hung inside this single room to form two separated rooms, but the Lord wanted His people to first understand that the tabernacle as a single, undivided room.

Why?

When we go back to the beginning of the Bible we see how the heavens and the earth were created. The Garden of Eden is called the Garden of God in other parts of the Bible[10] showing us that *originally* there was true harmony between heaven and earth.

The LORD God did not intend for heaven and earth to be divided from each other.

The Lord's intention is for heaven and earth to be united together in one. This is why He describes the tabernacle in this way. The creation was originally heaven and earth in harmony... one room, one 'space' without division.

So, after describing this tabernacle room the Lord asks Moses to "set up

---

[10] Ezekiel 28:13; 31:8-9.

the tabernacle according to the plan shown you on the mountain." It is almost as if He is asking His people to spend time thinking about each stage of the instructions, as if they were to meditate on what they had just made before moving onto the next section.

d. Then two rooms divided by a curtain (26:30-37)

After showing that the creation was once an undivided unity, then in the next section of instructions two things are added.

- The dividing curtain
- The altar of burnt offering

A curtain was hung to divide the tabernacle room into two parts. Thus an 'inner room' was sectioned off, a room that was shaped like a cube. The dimensions of that inner room were 15 feet by 15 feet by 15 feet (4.5 metres by 4.5 metres by 4.5 metres). The cube shape gives us a clue about the significance of that room. When we turn to the book of Revelation we find another cube-structure. In Revelation chapter 21 the apostle John was shown the City of God coming down to the earth. The angel with John shows him the measurements of the heavenly city:

> The angel who talked with me had a measuring rod of gold to measure the city, its gates and its walls. The city was laid out like a square, as long as it was wide. He measured the city with the rod and found it to be 12,000 stadia in length, and *as wide and high as it is long.* (Revelation 21:15-16)

The heavenly city is symbolised as a cube – just like this inner room in the tabernacle. This inner room was called the Most Holy Place and it represented heaven, divided from the Holy Place, the outer room, by a thick curtain.

The thick curtain is worthy of attention. In Exodus 26:31 the first thing we learn about this curtain is that it should have "cherubim worked into it by a skilled craftsman." The curtain displayed angels guarding the division between heaven and earth. This reminds us of Genesis 3:24.

> After he drove the man out, (the LORD God) placed on the east side of the Garden of Eden cherubim and a flaming sword flashing back and forth to guard the way to the tree of life.

So, the room representing heaven was cut off from the rest of the tabernacle area, symbolically guarded by the cherubim. Later we will see that only the high priest was able to go through that curtain.

We do have such a high priest, who sat down at the right hand of the throne of the Majesty in heaven, and who serves in the sanctuary, the true tabernacle set up by the Lord, not by man. Every high priest is appointed to offer both gifts and sacrifices, and so it was necessary for this one also to have something to offer. If he were on earth, he would not be a priest, for there are already men who offer the gifts prescribed by the law. *They serve at a sanctuary that is a copy and shadow of what is in heaven.* This is why Moses was warned when he was about to build the tabernacle: "See to it that you make everything according to the pattern shown you on the mountain." (Hebrews 8:1-5)

In Exodus 27:9-19 we learn that the tabernacle structure was located in a courtyard area, defined by a kind of fence. The fenced tabernacle area represented the whole creation, with the outer room (the Holy Place) representing the Church and the inner room (the Most Holy Place) representing Heaven itself.

With this model in mind, we should realise how it was teaching or prophesying the priestly work of Jesus the Messiah.

Remember that the curtain was installed to divide heaven away... but the altar of burnt offering was also given. The book of Leviticus begins by explaining to us that the burnt offerings make atonement for sin. So, the LORD did not want to place the curtain of separation without immediately also giving the Gospel hope of atonement. It reminds us of Genesis chapter 3. Even as He pronounced the curses caused by sin, yet He prophesied His own birth and victory over Satan (Genesis 3:15).

The thick curtain dividing heaven from the rest of the creation was torn down, from top to bottom, when Jesus made atonement for the sins of the world – see Matthew 27:51.

Hebrews chapter 9:6-12 puts the matter like this:

> When everything had been arranged like this, the priests entered regularly into the outer room to carry on their ministry. *But only the high priest entered the inner room, and that only once a year,*

and never without blood, which he offered for himself and for the sins the people had committed in ignorance. The Holy Spirit was showing by this that the way into the Most Holy Place had not yet been disclosed as long as the first tabernacle was still standing… When Christ came as high priest of the good things that are already here, *he went through the greater and more perfect tabernacle that is not man-made, that is to say, not a part of this creation*. He did not enter by means of the blood of goats and calves; but *he entered the Most Holy Place* once for all by his own blood, having obtained eternal redemption.

Tom Parsons, who has taught me so much about the tabernacle, describes the vision of the tabernacle like this:

The tabernacle was given as God's model of Moses' overwhelming visual experience whilst on Mount Sinai with the Lord in heaven. The apostle Paul saw heaven, but he was not permitted to relay his experience (2 Corinthians 12). Just consider the privilege of having a detailed description of the Most Holy Place! We can see into the dwelling of the Father.

But why does He give us such a vision? He shows us because eventually He wants His home to join with our home. He wants to dwell with us here on earth. Of course, sin gets in the way and that's why the Father cannot just move straight into the tabernacle. It was the Angel of the LORD who lived in the model with the ancient Church. He is the eternal mediator who represents the Father perfectly. His presence in the tabernacle was the perfect education in what it takes for the Father to dwell on earth. He is the perfect revelation of the Father.

Study 8   Bible Study Questions

Hebrews 9:23-28

The Tabernacle was not just teaching the Church general truths about heaven and earth. It was teaching about the future work of the Messiah.

1. Verse 23-24: What is the relationship between the *earthly* Most Holy Place and *heaven* itself?

2. Verse 24: Why has Christ been in the heavenly Most Holy Place for so long? Has something gone wrong?

3. Verse 25: Why did the priests of the copy have to keep repeating all their work?

4. Verse 26: Will Jesus ever have to come and die again?

5. Verse 27: Belief in re-incarnation is more popular than ever. How can we explain the truth to a person trapped by this idea?

6. Verse 28: Jesus will eventually return from His time in the heavenly Most Holy Place – what will happen then?

Study 8   Further Questions

1. There have been all kinds of books and studies of the Tabernacle down the ages – but not all have been very illuminating. Too often the writer sees wonderful things that nobody else can see! What is the remedy for such imaginative work?

2. We have seen that the curtain dividing the 2 rooms is not part of the basic plan of the Tabernacle – Exodus 26:1-30. How do you think heaven and earth were joined before the sin of Adam and Eve in Genesis 3?

Study 8   Daily Readings

Day 1	Exodus 35:4-29
Day 2	Exodus 35:30-36:7
Day 3	Exodus 27:9-19
Day 4	Exodus 26:1-30
Day 5	Exodus 26:31-27
Day 6	Hebrews 9:1-22
Day 7	Numbers 9:15-23

The daily Bible readings are an opportunity not only to read through all of the material in the book under study, but also to read parts of the Bible that relate to the themes and issues that we have been considering. We try to make sure that we receive light from the whole Bible as we think through the key issues each week.

The Mercy Seat

Study 9   The Furniture of the tabernacle

Key Truth: The Three pieces of Tabernacle furniture represent the three Persons who are the God of Israel.

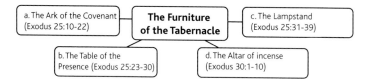

a. The Ark of the Covenant (Exodus 25:10-22)

The Furniture of the Tabernacle

c. The Lampstand (Exodus 25:31-39)

b. The Table of the Presence (Exodus 25:23-30)

d. The Altar of incense (Exodus 30:1-10)

a.   The Ark of the Covenant (Exodus 25:10-22)

The strangest thing about the instructions for building the tabernacle is that three pieces of furniture are described... *Before* the actual tabernacle itself!

If we remember that the tabernacle represents the creation – the heavens and the earth... then how can there be anything *before* that?!

How can anything be older than the heavens and the earth?

Well, the Father, Son and Holy Spirit are 'older' than the creation, so could these three pieces of furniture symbolise the Three Persons who are the Living God?

The Ark of the Covenant was a wooden box covered in gold. It had a special lid (called the Mercy Seat) and on the lid were two cherubim with outstretched wings. Inside this box were three items: the stone tablets of the 10 commandments; a jar of manna; and Aaron's budding branch.

The Ark of the Covenant was to be placed inside the Most Holy Place, the closed off inner room. In other words, the Ark of the Covenant was symbolically placed in heaven.

Although the ark was a box, yet in many ways we are to think of it as a *throne*. To choose just one example of this, in 1 Samuel 4 the people of Israel collect the Ark of the Covenant from Shiloh:

The people sent men to Shiloh, and they brought back the ark of the covenant of the LORD Almighty, who is *enthroned between the cherubim*. (1 Samuel 4:4)

The ark symbolised the throne of the Father in heaven. In both Daniel 7 and Revelation 4, we see that heaven is dominated by the throne of the Father.

As I looked, "thrones were set in place, and the Ancient of Days took his seat. His clothing was as white as snow; the hair of his head was white like wool. His throne was flaming with fire, and its wheels were all ablaze. A river of fire was flowing, coming out from before him. Thousands upon thousands attended him; ten thousand times ten thousand stood before him. The court was seated, and the books were opened. (Daniel 7:9-10)

In Revelation 4:1-3, the first thing that John sees is this throne, the throne from which all authority flows.

After this I looked, and there before me was a door standing open in heaven. And the voice I had first heard speaking to me like a trumpet said, "Come up here, and I will show you what must take place after this." At once I was in the Spirit, and there before me was a throne in heaven with someone sitting on it. And the one who sat there had the appearance of jasper and carnelian. A rainbow, resembling an emerald, encircled the throne.

The Ark of the Covenant, where the LORD sits enthroned between the cherubim, was a paradox. On the one hand, to go into the most Holy Place meant death because of the separation represented by the curtain. On the other hand, once a year, the lid of the Ark, the Mercy Seat, was sprinkled with blood to bring atonement and peace. The very fact that this lid was called the *Mercy* Seat shows this.

Tom Parsons, again, puts this so well:

God says in Exodus 25:22 that it is precisely there, "above the cover, between the two cherubim" that He will meet with humanity. That place of meeting and atonement, the lid of the Ark, is rightly called a *mercy* seat. It symbolically 'absorbed' the judgement of God so that there could be a meeting with humanity.

The Ark, and its Mercy Seat, presents the impossible possibility: the acceptance of sinners into the throne room of the Father. When Paul wants to teach the Romans how the Cross of the Messiah enables God to forgive guilty people, he refers them to the mercy seat, Romans 3:25. The mercy seat absorbs God's wrath, so sinners don't have to face it. The Father's throne of judgement is based in mercy.

b. The Table of the Presence (Exodus 25:23-30)

The two other 'eternal' pieces of furniture were to be placed in the outer room, the Holy Place. Bear in mind that the Holy Place represented the earth, and more specifically, the Church on the earth.

The table of the Presence was a wooden table overlaid with gold. It had special carrying poles and on the table were placed 12 loaves of bread. This "bread of the Presence" enables us to identify the significance of this item of furniture.

First, the word "Presence" is linked to the Angel of the LORD.

> The LORD replied, "My Presence will go with you, and I will give you rest." Then Moses said to him, "If your Presence does not go with us, do not send us up from here. How will anyone know that you are pleased with me and with your people unless you go with us? What else will distinguish me and your people from all the other people on the face of the earth?" (Exodus 33:14-15)

Notice that the Presence going with the people is the same as the LORD going with them.

> From heaven he made you hear his voice to discipline you. On earth he showed you his great fire, and you heard his words from out of the fire. Because he loved your forefathers and chose their descendants after them, he brought you out of Egypt *by his Presence* and his great strength... (Deuteronomy 4:36-37)[11]

Second, the bread itself has a special association with God the Son. Jesus Himself declared Himself to be the Bread of Heaven in John 6.

> I am the bread of life. Your forefathers ate the manna in the desert, yet they died. But here is the bread that comes down

---

[11] Compare this also to Judges 2:1-4

from heaven, which a man may eat and not die. I am the living bread that came down from heaven. If anyone eats of this bread, he will live for ever. This bread is my flesh, which I will give for the life of the world. (John 6:48-51)

c. The Lampstand (Exodus 25:31-39)

The golden Lampstand was a beautiful item. It was fuelled by olive oil to each of its seven branches. It had to be crafted in such a way that it looked almost like a golden plant with flowers and buds.

We should appreciate the significance of this oil. In the Scriptures three classes of person were anointed with oil: priests (eg Exodus 29:7); prophets (eg 1 Kings 19:16); and kings (eg 1 Samuel 10:1, note 1 Samuel 10:6, 10).

Why were they anointed with oil? To show that they needed the Holy Spirit to equip them for their work. Notice how David is anointed by Samuel to see the direct connection between the oil and the Spirit.

> Samuel took the horn of oil and anointed him in the presence of his brothers, and from that day on the Spirit of the LORD came upon David in power. (1 Samuel 16:13)

So, the fact that the Lampstand is fuelled by this olive oil is enough to make us think of the Holy Spirit. However, the Scriptures quite directly address the significance of this Lampstand. Consider this incident from the prophet Zechariah:

> Then the angel who talked with me returned and wakened me, as a man is wakened from his sleep. He asked me, "What do you see?" I answered, "I see a solid gold Lampstand with a bowl at the top and seven lights on it, with seven channels to the lights. Also there are two olive trees by it, one on the right of the bowl and the other on its left." I asked the angel who talked with me, "What are these, my lord?" He answered, "Do you not know what these are?" "No, my lord," I replied. So he said to me, "This is the word of the LORD to Zerubbabel: `Not by might nor by power, *but by my Spirit*,' says the LORD Almighty. (Zechariah 4:1-6)

In Revelation chapter 4:5 the seven lamps before the throne of God are identified as the sevenfold Spirit of God.

So, in the first section of the tabernacle instructions we have three pieces of furniture, each associated with a member of the Trinity. The three pieces of furniture come before the rest of the tabernacle to show that the Living God is eternal, not part of the heavens or the earth.

d. The Altar of Incense (Exodus 30:1-10)

There is one final piece of furniture that was placed inside the tabernacle – the altar of incense. This is not described till much later in the instructions, but we cover it at this point so that we can appreciate its place in relation to the Ark, the Table and the Lamp.

The altar of incense was to be placed just near to the dividing curtain in the outer room, the Holy Place.

This altar represented the prayers of the church.

> golden bowls full of incense, which are the prayers of the saints. (Revelation 5:8)

> My name will be great among the nations, from the rising to the setting of the sun. In every place incense and pure offerings will be brought to my name, because my name will be great among the nations," says the LORD Almighty. (Malachi 1:11)

Can we imagine the layout of the tabernacle with these four pieces of furniture positioned in it?

The altar of incense is positioned right in the middle of the other three! The prayers of the church are located in the very centre of the life of the Trinity. It is as if we are being told that the place of the Church is right in the centre of the life of God! How amazing!

Study 9   Bible Study Questions

Exodus 40:1-5, 17-33

The more we learn about the layout of the Tabernacle and its furniture, the more we will understand about the overall teaching of the Bible.

1. Verses 1-2: Why should the Tabernacle be setup on the first day of the first month?

2. Verse 3: The curtain was 'a shield' for the Ark. Why? Who was being shielded from what?

3. Verses 4-5: After the serious statement of the 'shield curtain' had been made, now the table and the lampstand are put in place. What impact would they have on those setting it all up?

4. Verses 17-32: What is the key phrase throughout this account?

5. Verses 30-32: We haven't studied the basin for washing in the notes, but what do you think it was teaching? See Titus 3:3-8.

Study 9   Further Questions

1. When we read the exciting stories about the Ark of the Covenant in 1 Samuel 4-6, we can see why it has inspired so much mythology and fantasy. However, what should we think about all these books and films about 'discovering' the Ark?

2. Could you use a plan or model of the tabernacle to explain the Gospel to someone? What would be the problems and what would be the advantages?

3. Where is the Ark of the Covenant now? (Revelation 11:19)

Study 9   Daily Readings

Day 1	Exodus 25:10-22
Day 2	Exodus 25:23-30
Day 3	Exodus 25:31-40
Day 4	Exodus 30:1-10
Day 5	Revelation chapter 4
Day 6	Zechariah 4:1-6
Day 7	1 Samuel chapter 5

The daily Bible readings are an opportunity not only to read through all of the material in the book under study, but also to read parts of the Bible that relate to the themes and issues that we have been considering. We try to make sure that we receive light from the whole Bible as we think through the key issues each week.

The High Priest

Study 10 The priests of the tabernacle

Key Truth: The priests of the Tabernacle teach us about Jesus, our great High Priest.

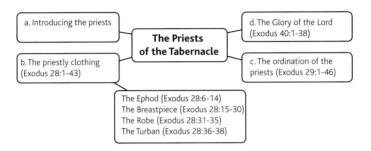

a. Introducing the priests

The Priests of the Tabernacle

d. The Glory of the Lord (Exodus 40:1-38)

b. The priestly clothing (Exodus 28:1-43)

c. The ordination of the priests (Exodus 29:1-46)

The Ephod (Exodus 28:6-14)
The Breastpiece (Exodus 28:15-30)
The Robe (Exodus 28:31-35)
The Turban (Exodus 28:36-38)

a.   Introducing the Priests

Let's take a moment to consider the picture of reality that has been provided by the tabernacle so far.

The heavens and the earth were intended to be a united single reality.

Human sin caused a division and we were driven out of the presence of God. Now there is wall of fire, guarded by the cherubim, preventing anyone returning to heaven.

Is there an answer? Is there a way back? We might want to cry out with Job:

> If only there were someone to arbitrate between us, to lay his hand upon us both, someone to remove God's rod from me, so that his terror would frighten me no more. (Job 9:33-34)

The world desperately needs a mediator. The whole creation desperately needs someone who is capable of tearing down the curtain, cleansing the universe, atoning for our sin and re-creating it all into a new unified whole.

There is such a Person: Jesus the Great High Priest of the whole creation, the only Mediator between God and humanity.

When we look at the priests in Exodus, with their garments and activities, we are being shown aspects of this Divine High Priest. The Lord God was explaining who He is and how He would accomplish the mighty work of redemption in His incarnation, life, death, resurrection and ascension.

b. The priestly clothing (Exodus 28:1-43)

At the beginning of the description of the priestly garments we are told something very important about them:

> Make sacred garments for your brother Aaron, to give him dignity and honour (Exodus 28:2)

These earthly shadows of the Perfect and Divine High Priest do not have the dignity and honour to perform their work… so they need to be clothed with these symbolic garments. Each of these items of clothing show us aspects of the dignity and honour of Jesus, the true High Priest.

Exodus 28:4 lists the clothes that had to be made:

- A breastpiece
- An ephod
- A robe
- A woven tunic
- A turban
- A sash

The Ephod (Exodus 28:6-14)

The ephod seems to have been a kind of beautifully crafted 'apron', made from gold thread woven into blue, purple and scarlet fine linen.

The key feature of the ephod is that it had an onyx stone on each shoulder. Each stone was engraved with six of the tribes of Israel:

> Aaron is to bear the names on his shoulders as a memorial before the LORD. (Exodus 28:12)

The priest was not just a private individual. With those black stones he was symbolically carrying all the people of God on his shoulders. When he offered the sacrifices before the LORD he was acting on behalf of the church.

Think of the heavy, heavy weight of our sin that was laid on the shoulders of Jesus as He went to the Cross:

> We all like sheep have gone astray, each of us has turned to his own way; and the LORD has laid on Him the iniquity of us all. (Isaiah 53:6)

The Breastpiece (Exodus 28:15-30)

On top of the ephod was a stunning breastpiece made of gold, linen and precious stones.

The most amazing thing about this breastpiece was the four rows of precious stones. Each stone represented a tribe of Israel:

> There are to be twelve stones, one for each of the names of the sons of Israel, each engraved like a seal with the name of one of the twelve tribes. (Exodus 28:21)

The priest had the names of the people over his heart.

Again, we are being told that the identity of the priest is completely bound up with the people he represents. It is no wonder that the Bible constantly emphasises that Christ and His people are one: He is the Head and we are His Body; His life is our life.

As Jesus sits at the right hand of His Father, our names are written over His heart. He is not a mere emotionless legal representative. No, He is the One who loves us with the greatest love, an infinite love.

Many people have tried to determine which of the stones belongs to which tribe of Israel. This is not an easy task, but here is a possible solution.

Row	Tribe	Stone
1	Rueben	Ruby
	Simeon	Topaz
	Levi	Beryl
2	Judah	Turquoise
	Issachar	Sapphire
	Zebulun	Emerald
3	Dan	Jacinth
	Naphtali	Agate
	Gad	Amethyst
4	Asher	Chrysolite
	Joseph	Onyx
	Benjamin	Jasper

The Robe (Exodus 28:31-35)

Under the ephod was a blue robe. The distinguishing feature of this robe was the hem. On the hem there were to be brightly painted pomegranates (blue, purple and scarlet), but between each of the pomegranates was to be a *golden bell*.

This 'musical' robe was to worn to indicate the priests presence before the LORD.

> Aaron must wear it when he ministers. The sound of the bells will be heard when he enters the Holy Place before the LORD and when he comes out, so that he will not die. (Exodus 28:35)

The sound of the golden bells as he walked meant that there was nothing secret or private about the work of the priest. In Leviticus 10 we see two priests killed when they wandered carelessly into the presence of the LORD. The golden bells were a audible warning that the priests were coming before the LORD God.

The worshippers outside, watching and praying around the tabernacle, would be able to hear the movements of the priests as they mediated for them.

The Turban (Exodus 28:36-38)

The priest's turban had a plate of pure gold attached to the front and on it were written the following words: HOLY TO THE LORD.

The priest was utterly dedicated to his job. Although all the earthly priests were sinful people, yet this golden sign was declaring that the promised Messiah-Priest would be truly and absolutely holy. The holy Messiah-Priest had no sin of any kind.

> It will be on Aaron's forehead and he will bear the guilt involved in the sacred gifts the Israelites consecrate, whatever their gifts may be. It will be on Aaron's forehead continually so that they will be acceptable to the LORD. (Exodus 28:38)

The symbolic holiness of the priest is what enables him to bear the sins of the people. When we think of Jesus we realise that if He had sins of His own, then He could not bear our sins: he would have had to pay for His own sins. However, because He was utterly holy, free from all sin, so He was able to take our sins and pay for them.

God made him who had no sin to be sin for us, so that in him we might become the righteousness of God. (2 Corinthians 5:21)

The same principle can be found in the Woven Tunic and Sash (Exodus 28:39-41). The Lord tells Moses: "make tunics, sashes and headbands for Aaron's sons to give them dignity and honour" (Exodus 28:40). The earthly priests were clothed with symbols of holiness, dignity and honour... but Jesus, the Eternal and Divine High Priest has all these qualities in Himself.

c. The ordination of the priests (Exodus 29:1-46)

Tom Parsons, again, expresses this best:

> Chapter 28 has presented a figure capable of entering into communion with the Trinity on behalf of others. But he is not yet ready for service. The priest cannot invite himself into the presence of God, he must be ordained. It is through his ordination that the LORD invites Aaron to minister before Him as High Priest. The rite of ordination (chapter 29) is intricate. Perhaps the two most striking features of this ceremony are the purification with blood and the anointing with oil, both full of Messianic significance.
>
> Blood flows everywhere in the ordination rite. It is sprinkled on the horns of the altar and poured at the base of the altar. Sacrifice underlies everything going on in the tabernacle.
>
> *Priesthood must be founded on sacrifice.*
>
> The priest's job is to bring the forgiven people into the presence of God. To keep himself in a state to gain forgiveness for others, Aaron had continually to offer sacrifices for himself. What a stark contrast that is to Jesus, who had no sins of His own that needed to be forgiven.
>
> Oil also gets everywhere – even over the beautiful garments. In 29:7, Aaron, in full regalia, is anointed with oil – the symbol of the Holy Spirit. This clearly prophesied the Messiah's life and work, who was filled with the Spirit without measure (John 3:34). The word Messiah literally means 'Anointed One'. Only a priest anointed with oil could serve in the Tabernacle.

d. The Glory of the Lord (Exodus 40:1-38)

The book of Exodus began in inglorious slavery and tyranny... and it ends with overwhelming glory and freedom.

> Moses set up the courtyard around the tabernacle and altar and put up the curtain at the entrance to the courtyard. And so Moses finished the work. Then the cloud covered the Tent of Meeting, and the glory of the LORD filled the tabernacle. Moses could not enter the Tent of Meeting because the cloud had settled upon it, and the glory of the LORD filled the tabernacle. (Exodus 40:33-35)

If we remember the symbolism of the tabernacle, that it represents the whole creation, then we see a wonderful prophecy here. If the glory of the LORD *filled* the tabernacle in this way, in such power that no sinful man, not even Moses, could enter it, then do we glimpse the future of the universe itself here? Will the glory of the LORD actually fill the whole creation with such power one day?

> the earth will be filled with the knowledge of the glory of the LORD, as the waters cover the sea. (Habakkuk 2:14)

Yes, a day is coming when the shadow of Exodus 40:33-35 will become solid and universal. The plan of redemption is written on a cosmic scale. Nothing less than the re-unification of heaven and earth as a new creation will satisfy our Glorious God.

> Then I saw a new heaven and a new earth, for the first heaven and the first earth had passed away, and there was no longer any sea. I saw the Holy City, the new Jerusalem, coming down out of heaven from God, prepared as a bride beautifully dressed for her husband. And I heard a loud voice from the throne saying, "Now the dwelling of God is with men, and he will live with them. They will be his people, and God himself will be with them and be their God. He will wipe every tear from their eyes. There will be no more death or mourning or crying or pain, for the old order of things has passed away." He who was seated on the throne said, "I am making everything new!" Then he said, "Write this down, for these words are trustworthy and true." (Revelation 21:1-5)

Study 10   Bible Study Questions

Hebrews 7:23-8:13

The Messiah is our priest. If we want to understand all that that means, we must pay careful attention to all that the Bible teaches us about the priests who looked forward to His coming.

1. Verses 23-25: Why is it so important that Jesus is immortal?

2. Verses 26-28: Make a list of all the qualities of Jesus the Great High Priest.

3. 8 verses 1-2: What is the significance of Jesus "sitting down" in the heavenly Most Holy Place?

4. Verses 3-5: What is the relationship between Jesus the Great High Priest and all the priests at the earthly Tabernacle?

5. Verse 6-13: What was so inferior about the covenant that lasted from Moses down to the death of Jesus?

Bookby**Book**

Study 10 Further Questions

1. Where else in Scripture do we see these 12 stones on the breastpiece and what might that teach us about their meaning?

2. What other kinds of people are anointed with oil in the Old Testament, and what else does this tell us about the Promised Anointed One?

3. The goal of the whole creation is for the Trinity to *come and live here* with us after the Resurrection at the return of Jesus. However, in most popular thinking, the idea is that we will all *go away* to where God lives and stay *there* forever. Why do you think there is such a gap between the Bible's teaching and popular opinion?

Study 10	Daily Readings
Day 1	Exodus 28:1-30
Day 2	Exodus 29
Day 3	Exodus 30:22-38
Day 4	Hebrews 4:14-5:10
Day 5	1 Samuel 2:12-36
Day 6	Exodus 40
Day 7	Revelation 21

The daily Bible readings are an opportunity not only to read through all of the material in the book under study, but also to read parts of the Bible that relate to the themes and issues that we have been considering. We try to make sure that we receive light from the whole Bible as we think through the key issues each week.

4 Suggested Answers to the Bible Study Questions

Study 1 Bible Study Answers

Exodus 1

1. They came as the family of Joseph, with great honour. Joseph created the power and wealth of Egypt because of the prophecies that the Lord gave to him.

2. All earthly glory, wealth and influence is fleeting. The world's honour does not last into eternity. It can be so tempting and yet we cannot love the world and God at the same time. Any power, wealth or honour that we have must be seen in the light of eternity and the glory of Christ. To know the Living God is beyond anything that the world can give.

3. In the Sermon on the Mount Jesus tells us to pray and give and live for the Unseen Father who is watching us. He sees what we do and will honour us for it. We can be of most help to the Christian church by walking the way of Jesus with all our heart, mind, soul and strength.

4. Pharaoh had no regard for human life. The midwives were ready to die in their obedience to the LORD.

5. God's approval meant far more to the midwives than their place in this passing age. Whether they lived or died did not matter so long as they were faithful to the Lord. When we trust Him and follow His ways we must be ready to face the same kind of rejection from the world as He did... but we will also know the wonderful acceptance and joy that He alone can give.

6. Both Moses and Jesus were pursued as babies by power-mad tyrants. Both Moses and Jesus led the people out of captivity and slavery. Moses great life work was a shadow or sign pointing forward to the ultimate rescue work of Jesus.

Study 2   Bible Study Answers

Exodus 4:1-17

1. The serpent represents the power of Satan with all his principalities and powers. The Lord has complete power over the devil and all his schemes. If we stand firm in the Lord then the devil cannot overcome us. The devil's work brought the world into captivity, sin and death. If the Lord can overthrow the devil then He can surely redeem us.

2. Picking up a snake by its tail is a very dangerous thing to do... yet it was unable to harm Moses.

3. We have very sinful hearts. When Moses puts his hand to his heart the condition of his heart is revealed. Yet, by the Lord's power this inner corruption can be healed. By His death and resurrection we can be born again, receiving new hearts.

4. The Egyptians worshipped the created gifts, but not the Creator who gave them. If they would only turn to Him then they could drink of the water of life that would satisfy their very deepest thirst.

5. The LORD Jesus has called us to follow Him and obey His commandments. He knows all about the specific situation of our lives. He knows where we live, our neighbours, our workplace, our abilities... yet He tells us to live His way and witness to Him. We may feel unable to do this, yet He is the Living Lord who created us. If we trust Him and step forward in obedience He will never let us down.

Study 3   Bible Study Answers

Exodus 5:1-6:1

1. This Pharaoh had forgotten that everything he owned and all the power and glory of Egypt had been graciously given by the LORD through Joseph hundreds of years before. This ingratitude is the constant danger of the sinful human heart.

2. Pharaoh claims not to know the LORD God, so Moses and Aaron tell him the key information. The terrible judgements of the LORD God would come unless He received the sacrifices of atonement. The same message holds today: the judgement of God is coming on the world and the only place of safety is the sacrifice of the Lamb of God.

3. The LORD says "go and have a festival". Pharaoh says " go and work much harder". The LORD is kind and generous, whereas sinful men are always ultimately cruel and heartless.

4. The Israelite leaders see themselves as Pharaoh's people rather than the Church of the Living God. Therefore, they are drawn into seeing life from Pharaoh's view rather than the LORD's.

5. We can see that they should have trusted in the Angel of the LORD to deliver them, but what about us? When we are going through the times of trial and suffering, we should remember that He has promised to be with us until the end of the world. As we cry to Him for strength and peace and joy, He will answer us. If we don't feel the answer as soon as we want, let's continue to trust Him that He will answer in the best way in His time.

6. The world will at best only tolerate us. Even in spite of all their compromise, yet Pharaoh still hated the Lord's people. As the Church they were a rejection of all that Pharaoh stood for. The more we resemble Jesus the more we will be rejected by the sinful human world. The closer we are to Jesus the more extreme and divided will be the world's response to us.

Study 4   Bible Study Answers

Exodus 12:29-42

1. The judgement of the LORD fell on anyone who refused to shelter under the blood of the lamb. Anyone could have escaped the judgement as long as they obeyed the Word of the Lord.

2. Note verse 39. Staying to wait for the bread to rise was a massive failure in priorities. When it was time to join the Lord's redemption, everything else had to be abandoned.

3. Nothing we possess now can be taken through death or into the new creation. Our money, our career, our house, our car and our status are all passing away. If we hang onto these things, investing our precious time in passing things, then we show that we are not really living for the new creation.

4. The Lord made the Egyptians willing to give these things. The Egyptian riches were to be used in the building of the tabernacle. Thus the tabernacle was actually made from the treasures of the Gentiles!

5. If the LORD could get so much money together so easily then we should never think that the Lord needs our money now. He has all the money in the world, but will allow us the privilege of joining in with His work. On the other hand, when we are in need of His resources, we can be completely sure that He can supply everything we need.

6. The Gospel is much bigger than any of us individuals. It is for every man and woman. It is for every age group, whether young or old. It is for every nation, not just for Jews. It even extends to the animal world. The Bible tells us that even animals will be present in the New Creation, as the lion lies down with the lamb.

7. How hard it must have seemed to think that the Word of the LORD was still relevant after so very long. it was spoken to a small nomadic family in a very different culture, but the Israelites had become a mighty nation of slaves in the world's superpower. Nevertheless, the book of Exodus tells us that the memory of Abraham, Isaac and Jacob was still alive in the church. They had not entirely forgotten.

Study 5   Bible Study Answers

Exodus 16:1-18

1. It might seem reasonable, yet it showed a terrible lack of trust. The Angel of the LORD had performed such mighty miracles to deliver them from Egypt... so surely He wouldn't abandon them in the desert. Grumbling means no trust.

2. He is wonderfully patient.

3. He wanted only blessing for them, but this would come only if they really trusted Him and obeyed His commands.

4. He wanted them to live in constant dependence on Him, on His promises. He did not want them to store it up, because then they would forget that they needed His provision every single day. Jesus taught us to pray every single day for our daily bread.

5. The manna was given... but merely eating the miraculous bread was not enough. It needed to be eaten with a heart full of trust and obedience if there was to be true fellowship with the LORD God. Jesus is the food that gives eternal life to us as we feed on Him.

6. The book of Exodus was written so that the Church in every age could be taught how to trust in Jesus and feed on Him. We feed on Jesus by believing on Him.

Study 6   Bible Study Answers

Exodus 24:1-18

1. It is the visible LORD, the Angel of the LORD, the pre-incarnate Christ.

2. They failed with the first two commandments. They followed a bull-god and made a idol to worship. Exodus 32:6 indicates that they also fell into immorality.

3. Blood is the ink of Scripture. The payment for sin is death... so this book of salvation from sin is drenched in blood. The debt of sin has to be paid in blood if there is to be peace and fellowship with the LORD God. Only the blood of Jesus is really able to pay for our sin.

4. The Visible God can mediate for us. There is fellowship with God after blood sacrifice. The goal of the Living God is to bring us into table fellowship with Him. This is almost a mini-picture of the marriage feast of the Lamb at the end of the world.

5. Nadab and Abihu were to die for their disobedience in Levitcus 10. People say that if only the Lord Jesus would appear to them, then they would believe in Him. The Bible shows us that this is not true. Many people saw the incarnate Jesus yet hated Him.

6. Joshua was with Moses as he went up the mountain. Was he with Moses the whole time? The basis of Joshua's great leadership is to be found in his spiritual preparation. He was first and foremost a man in deep fellowship with the LORD God.

7. The key to victory and blessing in the Christian life is to be as close to Jesus as we can. We should study His word all that we can. Spend time talking to Him. Put His words into practice in all we do. Sing of Him, speak of Him and enjoy Him.

8. Think how terrifying the mountain must have seemed — a fire raging on the mountain and Moses within it. Fear, wonder, amazement, curiosity. The Living God within the darkness and fire must be a Holy and Mighty God.

| Study 7 | Bible Study Answers |

Exodus 32:1-25

1. The terror of the raging fire on the mountain as the real and Living God manifested His presence was very hard. A comfortable, hand-made god that we can 'control' is more appealing to our sinful hearts.

2. Aaron was weak and followed the crowd (see Exodus 23:2). He should have preached the truth to the people and told them to trust the LORD.

3. They rejected the true God of heaven. They made gods of gold. They used tools in their work.

4. Sin is a very serious matter to Him. He particularly hates the fact that they have treated Him so badly after all the good He has done for them. Ingratitude lies at the heart of evil. But, we also see how the LORD is provoking Moses to plead for mercy.

5. Moses does not try to argue against the LORD God. Rather he pleads the name and promises and honour of the LORD. He pleads for mercy on the basis of the glory and honour of the LORD God. The Word of God has power with God, whereas our wisdom does not.

6. Right back in Genesis 3 we see how sin makes us try to shift the blame and lie. Sin corrupts and destroys our integrity. Sin has shamed and belittled Aaron.

7. When the Church falls into sin, the world notices. The world will tolerate its own sin, but it knows that we are supposed to show a different way. When we embrace sin we make our Gospel witness an empty shell. Our lives need to be examples of holiness, humility and grace. If we do sin then our response should be honesty and humility – never self-righteousness.

Study 8   Bible Study Answers

Hebrews 9:23-28

1. The earthly Most Holy Place was a symbolic copy of the heavenly reality. It was a kind of working diagram designed to convey the most important facts about the dwelling place of the Father.

2. He represents us in His Father's presence. As long as He is there we have free access in Him to the Father. When He finally comes out, it will be the end of this present order and the beginning of the new creation.

3. The animal blood could not take away sin, and the priests had to keep sacrificing for their own sins.

4. No. His death was sufficient to cover all sins in the world through the whole history of the world.

5. Death is not a mere transition to a different stage of human life, but a conclusion to this passing life. Death is final.

6. When the Great High Priest comes back out of the Most Holy Place He will bring the completed salvation to the rest of creation. Then the barrier between heaven and earth will be forever ended and a new order of creation will begin — where there is no more death, pain, sorrow or sin.

Study 9   Bible Study Answers

Exodus 40:1-5, 17-33

1. It is the beginning of the New Year. This has a symbolic sense of a brand new beginning, a new era. Also, the way the finished tabernacle is filled with the glory of God points towards the New Creation being filled with the glory of God.

2. The glory of the Living God is too great for us to bear. His holiness would destroy sinful human beings. Therefore the curtain is placed to separate us from the presence of the LORD God – for our own safety. If we were restored to heaven in our sinful state we would all be destroyed.

3. There must have been a deep sense of fear and awe. As these items were put in position and as the significance of each was contemplated and explained by Moses, surely a deep sense of worship must have fallen on these people.

4. "just as the LORD commanded him". Obedience to the LORD is essential to our eternal safety and happiness.

5. It was a sign of new birth, regeneration. After the sacrifice of burnt offering then there was a washing of renewal as the tent was approached.

Study 10 Bible Study Answers

Hebrews 7:23-8:13

1. The priests of the old system of law were mortal sinful men who could only minister for a few years. You could not place your eternal safety in their hands because they too would die and need a saviour.

2. Holy, blameless, pure, separate from sin, exalted over the heavens, no need of sacrifices for himself, perfect for ever.

3. This indicates that He has completed all His work. He does not need to make new offerings or plead a new argument. What He has done is the final and complete solution to the sins of the world.

4. They were like actors playing the role of someone else – and Jesus is that Someone. They were showing off shadowy aspects of His glorious perfections.

5. The system of Law given through Moses was just a temporary expression of the heavenly reality. The tabernacle system was given only as a teaching aid until the reality was accomplished by Jesus. Jesus' work is the concrete reality whereas the tabernacle system is actually just an insubstantial shadow. The difference is the difference between a shadow and a real, living person.